Introduction to Business

Introduction to Business

A Primer on Basic Business Operations

Patrice Flynn

 BUSINESS EXPERT PRESS

Introduction to Business: A Primer on Basic Business Operations
Copyright © Patrice Flynn, 2020.

First published in 2020 by
Business Expert Press, LLC
222 East 46th Street, New York, NY 10017
www.businessexpertpress.com

ISBN-13: 978-1-94999-148-2 (paperback)
ISBN-13: 978-1-94999-149-9 (e-book)

Business Expert Press Business Career Development Collection

Cover and interior design by S4Carlisle Publishing Services Private Ltd., Chennai, India

First edition: 2020

10 9 8 7 6 5 4 3 2 1

Printed in the United States of America.

Abstract

Do we need yet another textbook on business fundamentals when every publishing house has stacks of such books ready for sale? No, we do not need another *standard* textbook. What we need is a new kind of teaching tool that at once accommodates the modern-day classroom and exposes new century students to the contemporary world of global capitalism in which today's businesses operate.

In primer form, Dr. Patrice Flynn clarifies the *functional areas of business*, a term used to describe what every businessperson needs to understand to be successful, from entrepreneurship to small business development, legal structure, going global, finance, big data, marketing, management, and more. It provides professors with just the right amount of rigorous content for a single-semester course at a 2-year community college, 4-year college, and international university. Each chapter is a stand-alone document, corresponding to approximately 1 week of classroom time when supplemented with real-time business examples as illustrated.

This primer demonstrates how a master teacher teaches new century students, thus giving supremacy to pedagogy along with rigorous content. The primer can be used with both business students and the growing group of nonbusiness students interested in learning how business works before entering the world of work. Every student will come away not only with a sense of the business areas that pique their interest but also with a deeper understanding of business from which to craft next career steps.

Keywords

business enterprises; functional areas of business; commerce; global business; management; global capitalism; teaching business

Contents

Introduction

In your hands is a unique and timely new student-driven product with the following key characteristics.

- This is a **primer**, not a lengthy (and expensive) textbook.
- This primer presents the **functional areas of business**, a term used by businesspeople to identify the key topics all businesses must pay attention to in order to be successful (e.g., entrepreneurship, small business development, finance, going global, big data, marketing, management, and more).
- This primer is a **career teaching guide** to help students decide what aspects of business might be of greatest interest. My hope is that students utilize this text to advance their scholastic and subsequent career decisions.

This is not your standard textbook. It reverses the outdated model that presupposes that content-based textbooks guide good teaching. In reality, most textbooks do not aid in teaching but are simply an accoutrement that universities require professors to use. Much of what you will see in this primer reflects what I do in the classroom, thus giving supremacy to pedagogy along with content.

What else distinguishes this business primer from contemporary textbooks?

- The text is written in the **second person** to personalize learning and engage students who are interested in working for a business one day or perhaps starting their own business.
- The tone is **conversational** to capture the imaginations of students and to model the idea that learning is an interpersonal endeavor. In my classroom, all students play a part in the conversation, regardless of socioeconomic background, age, gender, race, ethnicity, or major.

- This primer assumes **no prior knowledge** of the *functional areas of business*; hence, anyone can jump in and benefit from the teachings.
- This primer is accessible to business majors as well as **nonbusiness majors** interested in understanding the world of business before graduating from college.
- The content of this primer and presentation style reflect my having taught this course live to more than 1,100 undergraduates over the past 10 years. **Student feedback** each term is consistently excellent and provides valuable reflections that I incorporate into my teaching and bring to this student-driven primer.
- This primer is unique in that it does not differentiate between business and **global business**. In the twenty-first century, all business books should acknowledge that no matter where we are geographically located or in what industry, our businesses are impacted by global capitalism in some manner. It no longer suffices to teach business fundamentals without a comprehensive presentation on how to globalize a business. As a veteran educator of modern business and a business owner, I believe that students no longer have the luxury of not thinking globally. Any successful business today will require some knowledge of the global nature of our work.
- In addition to my role as professor of business, economics, and international studies, I am a **businesswoman,** who for 20 years served as senior vice president for administration and finance and then chief executive officer (CEO) in the private business sector, where I had direct experience implementing each of the *functional areas of busine*ss presented in this primer. Students value my firsthand experience and candor regarding business practicalities as well as my ability to discern and sort through what is most important for undergraduate students to know.
- This primer brings to light cutting-edge business practices, leaving behind outdated concepts. The chapter on big data, for example, supplants twentieth-century marketing approaches with today's data-driven models developed Google, Facebook, and Amazon, where predictions about our human experience are bought and sold to "nudge" us toward certain behaviors.

- This primer is **not a polemic**. I have no political/social/economic agenda to convey to students and teachers; hence, this book presents the key *functional areas of business* without judgment or prejudice. I want students to understand how business is conducted—plain and simple—and to determine on their own accord which functional areas of business most interest them and why.
- A final attribute of this primer is that it is written by a **woman**. Few textbooks in business and economics are solely authored by women. Women see and experience the world of business differently from male colleagues; thus, this primer lends a unique perspective to students who will take this course. Supporting a female business professor lends credibility to New York's Business Expert Press, which understands it is time for a more pluralistic set of academic college texts in this day and age when inclusion matters in our collective efforts to facilitate learning for everyone.

Career Guide

Part of my job as a professor at a liberal arts college is to help advise business students. Over the past 10 years, I have advised more than 350 students. My advice is not limited to academic goals. If a student is willing, I am available to provide career and workplace guidance. I think I have been successful in guiding advisees and would like to think that I could do the same thing on a larger scale through this primer.

Too often, students tell me that they choose college courses by simply looking at the course catalogue and making selections based on a descriptive sentence that appears to be of interest. Given the cost of college today, this is an expensive and sometimes futile method of course selection, much less career exploration.

At the end of this primer, not only will every student come away with a sense of one or two business areas that pique their interests and could be pursued in subsequent semesters but also will be grounded in the *functional areas of business*. Regardless of which area of business one ultimately pursues, it is imperative that everyone who works in business grasps what a business is and how business is operationalized through the functional areas in the context of contemporary global capitalism.

Experience teaching the *functional areas of business* has taught me that **business and nonbusiness majors** benefit from learning about business fundamentals. Majors in biology, psychology, theology, philosophy, history, health and environmental sciences, music, education, performing arts, international studies, foreign languages, political science, accounting, finance, criminal justice, sociology, sport management, information systems, veteran affairs, and computer science sign up for my course. Some of their friends ask if they can sit in on my classes after hearing how much students are learning that informs their job search. Having nonbusiness students in the mix enriches our conversations and provides me with new insights into the value of studying contemporary business practices.

Students express a desire to graduate from college knowing a little about business because they recognize that we live and work in a global capitalist economy. I wholeheartedly agree and welcome all students—business and nonbusiness majors alike—to join me in an exciting adventure exploring the nature of business as we experience it in today's global economy, a subject I find endlessly fascinating!

Primer Structure

College students today are unlikely to purchase expensive business textbooks. Professors know that college classrooms today do not warrant selecting a lengthy textbook for a one-semester course in which fewer than half the chapters will actually be covered. The problem is that professors have a limited choice of business textbooks. This primer provides professors with the exact amount of information needed for an introductory one-semester business course.

The primer is organized into 12 chapters, each a stand-alone document, corresponding to approximately 1 week of classroom time when supplemented with real-time business examples. Following the introduction, Chapter 1 defines the commonly used terms *business* and *functional areas of business*, hence grounding students in the material to be examined in each subsequent chapter. Chapter 2 examines the broader economy in which businesses operates. Chapter 3 lays out three main business legal structures for students to consider when establishing a new business: sole proprietorships, partnerships, and corporations.

Chapter 4 explores ways that a business can grow domestically. Chapter 5 considers options for how a business can go global. Chapter 6 captures the essence of entrepreneurship and small business development. Chapters 7 through 9 explore the financial functional area of business, beginning with financial management, then equity finance and debt finance. Chapters 10 and 11 focus on the areas of big data, marketing, and public relations, all rapidly changing fields of study. Chapter 12 closes with business management, including the roles and functions required of effective managers, using all your new skills and knowledge on the functional areas of business presented in this book.

Lastly, this primer serves a broad audience of professors and students at 2-year community colleges, 4-year colleges, and universities around the world.

To professors who are teaching a course on the *functional areas of business*, feel free to present this material in your courses in any order that suits your teaching style and student body. Each chapter is a stand-alone document that can be inserted into your course curriculum as needed. The business statistics and cases reflect state-of-the art business practices as this primer goes to press. I wholeheartedly encourage you to find creative ways to interject your own insights on best practices as they continue to unfold in the ever-changing and exciting world of global business!

> This primer serves a broad audience of professors and students at 2-year community colleges, 4-year colleges, and universities around the world.

CHAPTER 1

The Functional Areas
of Business

A valuable starting point for anyone interested in learning about business is the examination of the *functional areas of business*, a term used by businesspeople and economists to describe the key domains that all businesses must focus on to be successful. Some of the functional areas of business include entrepreneurship, small business development, finance, going global, human resources, logistics, big data, marketing, and management.

Ultimately, if you are going to work in business, you must decide which *functional area of business* most closely matches your interests, skills, and knowledge. How do you know what aspects of business suit you best? What college business courses should you take to pursue your interests? Students tell me their usual approach is to look at the college course catalogue and make selections based on a course title or a descriptive sentence. Given the exorbitant cost of college today, this is an expensive and sometimes futile method of course selection, much less career exploration. This primer provides a solution to such a guessing game.

The information in this primer serves as a guide for college students who are contemplating going into the field of business and are not sure what courses to take. With the aid of this primer, students will be grounded in the *functional areas of business*. Students will come away with a sense of one or two functional areas that pique their interest and could be pursued in subsequent semesters.

Every student will complete this course of study with a deeper understanding of business from which to craft next career steps.

Every student will complete this course of study with a deeper understanding of business from which to craft next career steps.

In addition, students recognize that we all live and work in a global capitalist economy and might therefore benefit from studying the essence of business thinking and operations. Knowing the fundamentals of business helps us make more informed decisions in our daily capacities as (a) consumers of business products and services, (b) recipients of business micro-targeting and other forms of merchandising, (c) users of financial instruments, and (d) workers who report to a boss. Thus, I welcome business and nonbusiness students to use this primer to help navigate today's global economy, a subject that captures my imagination each day.

To begin, we start by giving meaning to the terms "business" and "functional areas of business."

What Is a Business?

We hear and use the term "**business**" often in daily conversation. We tell friends of our interest in studying business. We stream the nightly business news. We read the business section of newspapers and magazines. We follow business online news feeds. We hear about new business opportunities for summer jobs and paid internships. Business executives are regularly interviewed on mass media by journalists.

What Is a Business?

An organization
comprised of people
who produce goods and services
to sell
to earn a profit
distributed to stakeholders.

What is a business? Simply put, a business is an organization comprised of people who produce goods and services to sell to customers with the expectation of earning a profit to be distributed to stakeholders.

The business **organization** is our unit of analysis. An organization:

- Can be large or small;
- Can have any number of employees, from one to thousands;
- Can operate a single store or 10,000 stores;
- Can produce goods and services in any of the industries tracked by the U.S. Department of Labor; and
- Can employ workers from the hundreds of different occupations represented in the modern workforce.

The various types of business organizational structures in the United States provide the legal framework for commercial activities, as explored in Chapter 3.

A business is an organization comprised of **people** who are employed to help the entity achieve its goals. These people come from all different occupational and industrial backgrounds. Their levels of education vary from job to job as do the roles and functions performed for the business. Some people are employed as wage and salary workers, others as contractors, sole proprietors, or self-employed persons. As will be stressed in Chapter 12 on management, people make the business. If you are a people-person, you probably will do well in business. You may even choose to study human resource management or international management, which are specializations in business management.

What are the people who work in a business organization doing all day? They **produce products or provide services** that are unique to their business enterprise. Economists identify two types of products. The first is called "goods," which represent tangible items produced for sale to customers (e.g., robots, computer sensors, mobile devices, shoes). The second is called "services," which represent other products offered to customers (e.g., plumbing, roofing repairs, physical therapy, language translation, computer-brain interface surgery). As presented in Chapter 6, entrepreneurship is central to taking an idea and making it a reality.

The products produced by a business are intended to be **sold** to existing or potential customers. This is where workers skilled in sales, advertising, and merchandising come into the picture. As we all know, the job of a salesperson in the 2020s contrasts starkly with a sales job in the twentieth century due to the advent of electronic sales on networked digital platforms, known as e-commerce. If becoming a salesperson is of interest to you, take a careful look at Chapters 10 and 11 on big data and marketing to get a jump on this functional area of business.

The process of hiring people to produce products and services to be sold to customers is intended to earn the owners of the business a **profit**, defined as total revenues minus total costs. By definition, private for-profit businesses are in the business of making money, which is what differentiates business from the two other sectors of the U.S. economy: (a) the public sector and (b) the private nonprofit sector. If profit is your goal, the private for-profit business sector is where you belong. For-profit firms strive to find appropriate ways to grow their businesses and hence increase profits, as considered in Chapters 4 and 5. Financial mechanisms to secure adequate financing for such growth are explored in Chapters 7, 8, and 9.

Lastly, who gets to keep the profits earned by a business? By law, the profits are **distributed to the stakeholders** on record. As discussed in Chapter 3 on business structure, businesses that are set up as sole proprietors distribute profits to the single owner of the business. Those set up as partnerships distribute profits to the general or limited partners per the partnership agreement. Businesses set up as corporations have a fiduciary responsibility to distribute profits to all owners, including shareholders.

Examples of the Functional Areas of Business

Now that we have a clear definition of a business, let's look at some of the key functional areas of business. In this primer, the functional areas presented do not include all functional areas, but rather those my students and I have identified as the most valuable in the initial stages of considering a career in business. The functions presented will help you understand what is required to start and run a successful business.

Entrepreneurship and Small Business Development

Entrepreneurship is where business begins and may lead to the establishment of a new legal business entity. Small business development stems from an initial idea and develops into the design of a business plan, consultation with attorneys, registering the new entity with the U.S. Internal Revenue Service (if operating in the United States), and the establishment of operations.

For some students, owning and operating their own business is the goal. For others, finding an established business in need of one's skills and knowledge is the goal. In either case, it is valuable to understand the entrepreneurial nature of the business as envisioned by the person who created the enterprise and/or those who hold the responsibility for running the business day-to-day.

Finance

The securing, handling, and distribution of money is a central functional area for all businesses and requires in-depth knowledge of finance and accounting. Most business programs include courses in accounting to give students a grounding in best practices to account for financial flows, adhere to generally agreed-upon accounting practices, and disseminate financial information to stakeholders. Financial management entails establishing clear financial goals with business owners, drafting budgets, and securing financing, if needed. Both equity financing and debt financing options are potential sources of money to create, build, and grow a business.

Everyone entrusted with running a business, whether a business owner or an employee, benefits from understanding the financial and accounting functional areas of the firm.

Big Data

A new functional area of business introduced in the twenty-first century is big data, known also as data science or behavioral futures markets. With the advent of sophisticated computational hardware and software, businesses today control enormous virtual supply chains of behavioral data on customer preferences, emotions, purchases, life styles, interests, and more. Merchandisers have found ways to monetize these data for the benefit of the world's advertisers and others who pay for its prediction products that retain and attract more customers.

Big data insights build on the genius of the Ad Men of the twenty-first century and bring new meaning to merchandising. If you are interested in merchandising, the big data functional area is the best starting place for your studies.

Marketing and Public Relations

In addition to big data, merchandisers learn how to harness the four marketing Ps, namely place; product; price; and promotion to increase sales, revenues, and profits for the firm. In the past 10 years, options for novel places to sell products have exploded due to customers carrying devices that allow marketers to micro-target products directly to potential customers, regardless of where the person and the products are physically located. Increasingly, big tech will engage in behavioral modification to "nudge" us toward certain decisions and actions. It is predicted that soon there will be no price tags on merchandise on store shelves as AI-powered sensors and software will generate a unique price for each customer to be posted on the person's mobile device.

Unique pricing is made possible through big data, handheld devices, beacons, sensors, and predictive analysis, all of which you will study in your marketing courses. The vice presidents for public relations have their work cut out for them in today's 24-7 news cycle environment that demands increasing communication between business and society.

Going Global

The world of business has also changed significantly over the past 40 years as a result of businesspeople expanding their geographical purview to include all corners of the globe. Financing, for example, is no longer limited to the country in which a business is incorporated. The workforce is no longer limited to a local economy, as workers migrate across state and national borders. The supply of inputs to production moves across the six inhabited continents. Potential customers of products and services may live anywhere on Earth.

Today, 195 sovereign nations engage in $19.5-trillion worth of merchandise trade flows and $5.8 trillion worthy commercial services flow annually. Gross global production is valued at $80 trillion. As more and more businesses enter the global business arena, earth-shattering global supply chains and infrastructure systems are constructed that defy traditional notions of operations and logistics.

In this primer, I argue that students no longer have the luxury of limiting their view of business to a single domestic economy. We all are best served by understanding the global interconnections of contemporary commerce. Hence, going global is a vital functional area of the firm to help your business grow and prosper.

Management

Last but not least, management has and always will be a central functional area of business given the all-important role that people play in reaching business goals. Human resource specialists examine the educational backgrounds, skills, and knowledge workers acquired over their work lives and try to match those abilities with the needs of business. Labor contracts, wages, compensation, expectations, and performance are examined in this functional area.

Every manager benefits from learning how to facilitate the ongoing process of harnessing and guiding people and other resources to achieve specific business goals. If you choose to take specialized business management courses, you will learn how to be an effective manager vis-à-vis the functions and roles you play as a manger.

Wrap Up

The above represents some of the key aspects of business that every businessperson needs to understand in order to appreciate the comprehensiveness of what we call **business**. While not all of the *functional areas of business* are covered in this primer, students will come away with a solid understanding of the key functional areas that will help guide their careers and future course of study.

CHAPTER 2

Business and the Economy

The United States is the largest economy in the world. In 2019, the Bureau of Economic Analysis reported that real gross domestic product—the value of all final U.S. goods and services produced—topped $20 trillion. The only country that comes close to this figure is the People's Republic of China, with a $14-trillion economy.

Every aspect of business is impacted by the economy in which we operate. Thus it is valuable to understand the size and scope of the domestic economy and how economic factors might impact your business.

Below we will explore two key concepts to help you consider how your business fits into the economy: the competitiveness continuum and the business cycle.

Competitiveness Continuum

There are hundreds of industries in the United States, from automobiles to data platforms, insurance, education, oil and gas, real estate, finance, construction, textiles, steel, and more. The best place to begin your job quest is to decide which industry captures your interest. This is a personal decision that will require research on what you can expect to be doing if you pursue a job and/or start a business in a particular industry.

Once you have honed in on a particular industry, the next thing to explore is the degree of competition within that industry. **Competition** is a central theme in business and is embraced by businesspeople on the road to success. A risk-averse person may not find success in business, but a person who thrives on competition will most likely succeed.

Before you launch your new business or go to a job interview, examine where your industry fits on the competitiveness continuum.

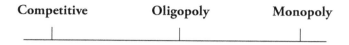

On the far left of the competitiveness continuum are the highly competitive industries with an array of business activities, featuring numerous producers and sellers. Competition at this end of the continuum is intense; to succeed, these businesses must ensure a wide variety of choices for consumers. In contrast, on the far right of the competitiveness continuum are industries with little to no competition. When one business dominates the industry, this is referred to as a **monopoly**.

In the twentieth century, the United States saw the rise of three monopolistic industries. Case one was Standard Oil, founded by John D. Rockefeller, which faced national scrutiny for being a monopolist in the crude-oil industry and was forced to break up in 1911. The second case occurred when AT&T (American Telephone & Telegraph) was forced to break up in 1984 for exhibiting monopoly power in the communications industry. The third case arose when Microsoft was deemed a monopoly in the computer industry in 1999 and forced to allow non-Microsoft browsers to run on its operating system.

Talk of a fourth case of monopoly today involves the ubiquitous Amazon.com Inc. (Amazon), founded by Jeff Bezos in 1994, which now dominates the e-commerce industry. Other possible monopolies include Facebook's dominance of the social media industry, Netflix's dominance of premium video-streaming, and Google's dominance in behavioral futures markets. Together, the five biggest U.S. digital platform technology businesses produce about a tenth of all corporate profits (i.e., Alphabet/Google, Amazon, Apple, Facebook, and Microsoft), leading competitors to call for anti-monopoly policy measures.

In the middle of the competitiveness continuum is a set of industries where only a few businesses operate, known as **oligopolies**. Examples of U.S.-registered oligopolistic industries include automobiles (e.g., GM and Ford), pharmacies (e.g., CVS-Aetna, Walgreen Boots Alliance, Rite Aid, and Walmart), wireless carriers (e.g., Verizon, AT&T, and Sprin-T), car rentals (e.g., Hertz, Avis Budget, and Enterprise), soft drinks (e.g., Coca-Cola and Pepsi), airline manufacturing (e.g., Boeing and Airbus), health insurance (e.g., Cigna, Kaiser Permanente, and WellPoint), and artificial intelligence (e.g., Alphabet, Amazon, Apple, Facebook, IBM, and Microsoft).

Knowing the competitive nature of the industry in which you plan to work or start a business is key to success. One of the biggest changes regarding the competitiveness continuum in the United States thus far in the twenty-first century is the growing concentration of businesses within industries, making it ever more difficult for new small business owners to break into selected industries. Specifically, we see fewer industries exhibiting competitiveness and more industries exhibiting oligopolistic-cum-monopolistic traits. The more concentrated an industry, the harder it is for new business owners in that sector to be successful.

As a result, when a foreign business bids to consolidate with a domestic business via a merger or acquisition, a proposal must be submitted to the Committee on Foreign Investment in the United States (CFIUS), a public sector agency under the U.S. Treasury. If CFIUS suspects the merger could significantly curb competition to the detriment of a U.S. business, the deal may be put on hold for further negotiations or rejected outright.

In 2018, several such cases were triggered when Chinese firms expressed interest in acquiring U.S. businesses but were turned down by CFIUS. For example, **Ant Financial**—the online payment service affiliate of e-commerce giant Alibaba—was turned down when it offered $1.2 billion to purchase MoneyGram International, a money-transfer business whose board of directors had approved the Ant Financial bid. CFIUS blocked the deal on January 3, 2018, on the grounds that the merger created a risk that the Chinese firm would be in a position to secure financial data on American soldiers and their families facing financial difficulties who could be possible espionage targets.[1] The ruling came as a surprise given that Ant

ANT FINANCIAL

---

[1]The Economist. January 6, 2018. "Ant Financial and MoneyGram Blocked Transfer," p. 46.

Financial was already engaged in an approved partnership with U.S.-owned VeriFone and First Data Corporation.

Numerous other proposed Chinese acquisitions have been denied by CFIUS based on broad concerns about Chinese acquisitions of American intellectual property, including China-based Canyon Bridge Capital's bid for Lattice Semiconductors, China Oceanwide Holding's bid for Genworth Financial, and China's HNA Group's bid for SkyBridge Capital. These cases are reminders to be vigilant of the connection between business and geopolitics anywhere on the planet, especially in the context of economic competition.

Business Cycle

Businesspeople track an array of key economic indicators from which to assess their own well-being in the context of the larger economy in which we conduct business. One such economic indicator is known as the business cycle, representing the ebbs and flows of a nation's economy.

The business cycle is divided into four parts: **expansion, peak, contraction,** and **trough**. An expansion is when an economy is experiencing an upswing during which we would expect to see rising output, income, employment, industrial production, and wholesale-retail sales. The peak is when an economy reaches a relative high before moving into a contraction, or downturn, with an expected drop in output, income, and employment. The trough is a relative low in the business cycle, indicating a turn from a contraction into an expansionary period.

The entity entrusted with tracking the U.S. business cycle is the National Bureau of Economic Research (NBER), a nonprofit organization established in 1920 in Cambridge, Massachusetts. Its charge is to carefully examine myriad data on the U.S. economy and determine where the economy is located on the business cycle. The NBER's most recent announcement on the business cycle was on September 20, 2010, when it reported that the last trough occurred in June of 2009.

Becoming aware of where the United States stands in the business cycle is critical for business success. Choosing to open your business at a time when the economy is shifting from a peak into a contraction could yield significantly different results than opening a business when the economy is shifting from a trough into an expansion. Moreover, how a business responds to changes in the business cycle depends on its industry. Some industries may perform poorly during contractions (e.g., restaurants) relative to others that may perform better during contractions (e.g., grocery stores), depending on the needs of consumers and their disposable income. Become aware of the preferences and behaviors of customers in your industry in anticipation of business cycle fluctuations.

Wrap Up

Context is everything! While you will do all within your power to ensure that your business is on top of its game, there will be times when the larger forces of an economy dominate your decision-making capabilities. For this reason, it helps to know a bit about the economy in which your business operates to understand aggregate economic trends as it impacts your success. A good starting place is to become familiar with the competitiveness continuum and business cycle, the focus of most daily business news feeds.

CHAPTER 3

Business Legal Structure

Once you gain a sense of the larger economy in which businesses operate and have a clear understanding of where your industry sits on the competitiveness continuum, it is time to decide how to set up your business. This is a legal matter that hinges upon the laws in whatever nation and state you want to conduct business.

Structure is captured in the first part of our answers to the question, "What is a business?" Specifically, business begins with the establishment of a particular **organizational type** or **legal structure**. To help you consider which business structure might best suit your needs, this chapter presents the major business types in the United States: sole proprietorships, partnerships, and corporations.

What Is a Business?

An organization
comprised of people
who produce goods and services
to sell
to earn a profit
distributed to stakeholders

You already made an important choice vis-à-vis organizational structure when you decided to create a private for-profit business as opposed to a public-sector agency or a private nonprofit organization. Within each of these three sectors of our economy, the kinds of entities that are legally permitted vary considerably. In the public sector, for example, a variety of governmental entities exist at the national, state, city, and municipal levels. In the private nonprofit sector, the U.S. Internal Revenue Service (IRS) ascribes more than three dozen different types of nonprofit entities.

Choices within the private for-profit business sector are somewhat simpler, with three basic forms, specifically **sole proprietorships**, **partnerships**, and **corporations**, each of which is described below, followed by a discussion of their relative size and advantages.

The choice of business structure depends on your specific industry, business model, and financial goals. If you plan to own, operate, and finance your business without external influence, you will likely establish your firm as a sole proprietorship, which is the most common type of business in the United States based on the number of business entities registered with the IRS. If you want to own, run, and finance your business with other people, a general partnership may be most suitable. If you are seeking to ultimately sell your business or grow to a size whereby most of the functional areas will be run by hired employees or subcontractors, you most likely will want to consider establishing your business as a corporation.

Initially, do not be overly concerned about choosing just the right type of organizational structure for your business. U.S. law is such that you may change your legal business type if you deem it valuable over time, one of the reasons we like to conduct business in the United States!

Type 1: Sole Proprietorships

Imagine watching an old spaghetti Western movie in which someone walks into a saloon and demands to speak to the proprietor of this establishment. With whom does the person want to speak? Historically, the answer is the owner of the saloon, who is entrusted with making most if not all of the decisions regarding this particular establishment.

We do not usually hear people use the old seventeenth-century English term "proprietor" any longer. In modern times, if a person wants to speak to someone who can help with a problem at a particular business establishment, one asks to speak to either the manager or the supervisor on duty.

The term "sole proprietor," although linguistically outdated, is still used to identify a specific type of business for legal purposes. The term "**sole**" suggests that there is one owner of the business. The term "**proprietor**" refers to the person in charge of the business, in this case the owner. Hence sole proprietorships are businesses owned and operated by a single person who has full responsibility for business activities and outcomes. The sole proprietorship exists until the owner shutters the business or dies.

Some sole proprietorships begin as small business easily managed by a single person, but over time may grow into large enterprises that require rethinking the legal structure of the business. Consider the individual named **Sam Walton**, who first learned the retail trade when he bought a franchise license in 1945 and successfully operated a Ben Franklin variety store in Newport, Arkansas. Walton parlayed his newly honed skills into his own store in Bentonville, Arkansas, called the Walton's Five and Dime that opened on May 9, 1950. Twelve years later, Walton owned and operated 16 retail stores and decided to open what he called the Walmart Discount City store in Rogers, Arkansas, on July 2, 1962, thus forging his unique one-stop retail business model that fundamentally changed commerce in rural and suburban America.

WAL★MART®
ALWAYS LOW PRICES.
Always.

Over time, Sam Walton became the primary stakeholder in the largest retail corporation in the world, Walmart Inc. By the time of his death in 1992, there were 1,960 Walmart stores worldwide, a number that has since risen to 6,363.

Think about the cartoon artist named **Walt Disney**, who drew cartoons in his garage in Kansas City, Missouri, a space shared with a mouse who inspired a famed Disney character. Disney first began to

achieve modest success after teaming up with his business-minded brother, Roy, to form the Walt Disney Company in Los Angeles, California, on October 16, 1923. Since those early days, the sole proprietorship transformed into the Disney Brothers Cartoon Studio in 1928, with Walt and Roy as equal partners, and ultimately the world's largest entertainment empire, the Walt Disney Company, long outliving the Disney brothers.

Think about the man named **Henry Ford**, who was a machinist and engineer working in Detroit, Michigan, in the years leading up to the advent of the automobile. To distinguish himself, Ford built a quadricycle, a gasoline-powered horseless carriage in the shed behind his home in 1896. Seven years later, he established the Ford Motor Company, made famous by operationalizing Frederick Taylor's assembly line, a mass production process that reduced the time it took to assemble one Model T from 12 hours to 90 minutes. His business persisted despite the drop in the number of U.S. carmakers from some 500 in 1900 to 200 in 1908.

Henry Ford's business is now a global automotive enterprise led by Henry Ford's great-grandson, William Clay Ford Jr., executive chair of the Ford Motor Company, one of only two remaining U.S. carmakers. The Ford Motor Company continues to demonstrate its ability to withstand the forces of global capitalism. In the depths of the Great Recession, Ford's stock price hit a low of $1.01 on November 20, 2008.[1] By 2017, its profit rose to $8.4 billion on $156.8 billion in revenues and closed the year with a stock price of $12.49.

As the Ford Motor Company and others illustrate, just because you start your business as a sole proprietorship does not mean you must retain this type of business structure forever. History reveals many cases of small

[1]B. Hoffman. 2012. *American Icon: Alan Mulally and the Fight to Save Ford Motor Company* (New York, NY: Crown Business).

business owners whose sole proprietorships grew to become either part-nerships, corporations, and/or transnational corporations. In the United States, it is fairly easy to change your business structure if that is desirable to meet your operational needs and long-term vision.

Sole proprietorships operate across a variety of industries, including res-taurants, bakeries, gift shops, retail stores, professional services, family-owned farms, and more. In fact, of the 115 industries the U.S. Department of La-bor's Bureau of Labor Statistics (BLS) has tracked since the 1930s, most have been dominated by sole proprietorships, at least when initially created.

The BLS classifies each business into the industry in which it is primarily engaged, alongside establishments doing similar things in similar ways. The North American Indus-try Classification System (NAICS) changes as new industries emerge over time, most recently cyber security, forensic accounting, and data science.

The current NAICS coding structure, in-troduced in 1997, classifies economic activity into 20 major industrial sectors.

- Five sectors are goods-producing enterprises (i.e., natural resources; agriculture, fishing, forestry and hunting; mining, quarrying, oil and gas extraction; construction; and manufacturing).
- Fifteen sectors are service-providing enterprises (i.e., wholesale trade; retail trade; transportation and warehousing; utilities; in-formation; finance and insurance; real estate and rental and leas-ing; professional, scientific, and technical services; management of companies and enterprises; administrative and support and waste management and remediation services; education and health ser-vices; health care and social assistance; arts, entertainment, and rec-reation; accommodation and food services; and all other services).

Statistics on Sole Proprietorships

How many sole proprietorships are there in the United States and how much money do these businesses bring in? Up-to-date statistics on

business activities are published on a regular basis by the U.S. Internal Revenue Service. The IRS collects data each year directly from private for-profit businesses, then verifies, collates, and releases the numbers in the *Statistics of Income (SOI) Bulletins* every quarter (winter, spring, summer, and fall). Because the most recent data are provided on a rolling basis from active, registered businesses, the IRS continuously updates the official data counts. Thus, do not be surprised if you see differences in initially released statistics and later bulletins.

The SOI statistical data collection effort dates back to 1916, providing us with more than a century of historical data on business activities in the United States by type of entity. For our purposes, we will examine three key pieces of information that are regularly reported in the *SOI Bulletins*: the number of business entities by type that are registered with the IRS, the annual receipts of these entities in U.S. dollars, and the annual net income in U.S. dollars.[2]

Table 3.1 presents a summary of the most recent data available on sole proprietorships in the United States. Notable is the fact that there are more than 25.5 million sole proprietorships registered with the U.S. Internal Revenue Service that have the legal right to conduct business in the United States as reported in 2019. These businesses brought in $1.42 trillion in receipts through the production and sale of goods and/or services. After all vendors, employees, and others who are owed money were paid, sole proprietors netted $328 billion as of 2019, a handsome profit.

[2]For additional numeric and descriptive data on U.S. businesses, see www.IRS.gov/taxstats.

Table 3.1 Statistics on sole proprietorships

Number of Entities	25,525,900
Receipts (USD)	$1.42 trillion
Net Income (USD)	$328 billion

Source: U.S. Internal Revenue Service. 2019. *SOI Bulletins: Summer 2019.*

Why Start Your Business as a Sole Proprietorship?

Given that 25.5 million businesspeople chose to start their businesses as sole proprietorships, it is worthwhile to examine some of the advantages and disadvantages of running a sole proprietorship.

One of the key benefits of a sole proprietorship is that it is **easy to start**, relative to other business types. You do not need to hire (and pay) an attorney to legally set up your sole proprietorship, although this option is available if you like. In the course of this primer, you will learn how to register your business with the IRS by yourself, hence, saving money and time immediately. It is also quite easy to obtain a license (or permit) to conduct business in your state, as required by law.

Even if you do not want to register your business with the IRS, you can still conduct business in the United States. By default, the IRS will treat any income (and loss) attributed to your commercial activities as it does for registered sole proprietorships. Moreover, sole proprietorships do not require charters or registration with the secretary of state in the state where you conduct business.

Sole proprietorships are **inexpensive to start** as you have the option of starting small (i.e., small inventory, small or no paid staff, and no lawyers). Sole proprietorships are also **easy to close** should you decide at some point that business is not the career path for you. All you are required to do is send a letter to the IRS with notification that you are no longer going to be in business as of a specified date. Of course, you cannot walk away from any outstanding obligations or debts, the latter of which must be paid even if you shutter your business, as will be discussed in the chapter on debt financing.

Those who decide to establish a business as a sole proprietorship also benefit from the privileges accorded to the business owner. For example, you get to make all the decisions, a benefit that may be one of the main reasons you are going into business in the first place. You also get to keep all the profits, once suppliers and all other stakeholders are paid, of course. With sole proprietors, there are no partners who will demand a cut of the profits.

One other advantage of owning a sole proprietorship is the **ease of reporting earnings and paying taxes** to the IRS. Sole proprietors are required to report to the IRS their business revenues, expenditures, net income, and/or losses by April 15th of each year. These data are reported on the standard U.S. Individual Income Tax Return, IRS Form 1040, which every adult in the United States must complete and submit annually.

On the IRS Form 1040, sole proprietors complete Line 12, denoting "Business income or (loss)," and attach details of business revenues and expenditures for the year on Schedule C (or C-EZ). There are no additional IRS forms to be completed, making annual tax filings straightforward for owners of sole proprietorships.

This easy way to file taxes for sole proprietorships reflects the U.S. ethos of supporting small businesses and making operating a business easy. By allowing business owners to report business income (or loss) on the IRS Form 1040, the income (or loss) is treated as a passthrough, meaning there are no additional business taxes owed to the U.S. Department of the Treasury, such as corporate income taxes that must be paid by businesses legally established as corporations as discussed below. Business profits are taxed at the individual person's personal tax bracket like wage and salary income.

Downsides of Sole Proprietorships

There are several disadvantages to be aware of if you are going to establish your business as a sole proprietorship. It is very important, for example, that you fully understand that as the sole owner or proprietor of the business, you are 100 percent responsible for everything that happens in the business. You cannot pass off responsibility to one of your employees on the grounds that you were not aware of what the employee was doing. You cannot walk away from any debts because you do not have the money to repay money owed. This concept is identified by lawyers as **unlimited liability**, meaning you have full responsibility for the activities of the business.

For example, as a sole proprietor, you are responsible for injuries suffered by customers and other visitors to your place of business if the injury suffered is the fault of your business. If, for instance, a business you own has a floor in need of repair and a customer's leg falls through the floor, resulting in serious injury, your individual assets could be at risk if the injured party wins a civil judgment for negligence against you as the sole proprietor.

Suppose, furthermore, that your sole proprietorship does not take in sufficient revenues to pay expenses, resulting in one of your suppliers not being paid. If this persists for a while, you may decide to close the business and declare bankruptcy. According to U.S. law, bankruptcy does not mean that you personally can walk away from the debt of a sole proprietorship. In fact, a sole proprietor is personally liable for any and all outstanding debts of the sole proprietorship even if the business closes its doors.

Similarly, if the business closes down and there are outstanding debts yet to be paid, you personally may be sued for repayment through a civil lawsuit against you as the owner. In this case, any remaining business assets (e.g., your store, office, warehouse, inventory, automobiles, computer devices, supplies, etc.) may be seized as well as your personal property (e.g., your home or car). In other words, **a sole proprietorship's debt is also your personal debt** if you are the owner of the business.

Another disadvantage to be aware of is that a sole proprietor assumes all the **risks** of running a business. There are no partners or board members sharing the risk.

Business is not for people who are risk averse; businesspeople are by nature risk-takers who benefit during the good times and pay the price during bad times.

Also important to consider when establishing a sole proprietorship is **access to financial capital** to start and/or run your business. As the sole owner, for example, it may be difficult to secure external financing because only one owner is committing to repaying a loan secured from a bank. In this case, the banker will review your financial documents and determine how much money you are likely to be able to repay on your own. If you had a couple of partners, the banker might be more likely to offer a larger loan, confident that three people will have a better chance of repaying the loan rather than only one person.

One other disadvantage to note here is that when you establish a sole proprietorship, there is **no division of labor**. Running the business, at least initially, is a one-person show. You are the person to get up early and open the doors to your store and stay until the last customer leaves in the evening. You must order and track inventory. You must meet and work with customers. You are the bookkeeper and accountant. You are the chief salesperson and merchandiser. In other words, you are responsible for running all the functional areas of your business.

Depending on the industry you are in and the size of your endeavor, being a one-person show may suit your needs quite well. My noting some of the disadvantages is not to discourage you from starting your business as a sole proprietor, but rather to give you a heads-up on the things to be considered ex-ante, that is, before you venture out on your own.

In sum, running a sole proprietorship can be extremely gratifying and lucrative as those of us who own businesses can attest. It can also be exhausting and trying at times. The trade-off between the advantages and disadvantages of owning and running a sole proprietorship can only be determined by you based on your unique business model, short- and long-term plans, and personality. Consult your most valued professors, mentors, and family members to help you sort through your options and inform your ultimate decision about setting up a business on your own.

Type 2: Partnerships

A second type of business structure in the United States is a partnership, enabling you to consider the possibility of going into business with one or more other people. While some entrepreneurs strive to start and run their own enterprise, others go into business with the expressed desire to work with others who share a common goal, vision, and business interest, in which case a partnership may be worth considering.

Partnerships are **voluntary associations**, meaning each person engaged in the partnership must agree to working with the other partners. Just because you may be very close to possible partners, for example siblings, it is unlawful for someone to list your name on a partnership agreement without your written consent. Hence the voluntary nature of all business partnerships.

To form a partnership, at least two people must agree to work together. But the ultimate number of partners is up to you to decide. Remember that whoever you include in the partnership will be a co-owner of the business. If just two of you start the partnership, you split things two ways; if there are 15 partners, you split things 15 ways. While each partner is valued because s/he brings some resources to the business, it is important to remember that as the number of partners increases so does the time required for effective decision making, which may or may not be a detractor to your mind.

The key to choosing partners is the **pooling** of skills, knowledge, experience, contacts, money, time, energy, creativity, knowledge of the world, and anything else a potential partner may offer. Choose partners who will bring something that you cannot offer, hence building a strong group of diversified owners who can work together.

It is easy for us to think about creating a business partnership with people who are similar to us, such as people with whom we grew up, went to college, were members of the same sorority, frequent the same bar or church, played on a sports team, or share the same interests. While it is great to be able to work with people who have shared experiences, this may not be to your advantage from a business perspective. Perhaps you could partner with people who have different life experiences, cultural backgrounds, and skills to diversify and strengthen your partnership.

In what industries do we tend to see partnerships? Most often, lawyers will establish their law practices as partnerships, identifying the key and/or founding partners in the name of the firm. Similarly, certified public accountants (CPA), medical doctors, private equity firms, real estate agencies, and advertising agencies are likely to form businesses as partnerships. Because businesses owned by spouses do not qualify as sole proprietorships, family businesses are likely to be set up as partnerships.

Articles of Partnership

If you decide to establish your business as a partnership, the first step is to create a legal contract, known as the Articles of Partnership. The document serves as an official agreement between all of the partners regarding selected elements relevant to the business. Some of the key elements to include in a partnership agreement include the date the partnership commences, the names of the partners, the name of the business partnership you are establishing, the location of the business, the purpose of the partnership, a sunset clause articulating when and how the partnership will be terminated, the initial amount of cash each partner puts into the business, the salaries to be paid to each partner, and the share ratios each partner may claim from the profits (and losses).

It is up to you and your partners to determine these parameters. For example, even though each partner may initially contribute different sums of money to establish the business, you may determine that the profits and losses be shared equally. When calculating distribution shares, be sure to factor in the sum of all the resources, work, and know-how contributed to the business by each partner. While one person may have more money to initially invest in the business, another partner may have much more experience in this industry and time to invest in the business. There are trade-offs to be considered among the partners to establish terms that are acceptable.

Make an effort to specify as many potential differences among partners at the outset to avoid having difficulties in the event the partnership dissolves unexpectedly. I suggest a relatively short sunset clause in the event the partnership does not unfold as expected. If you have a clause that specifies that the duration of the partnership agreement be for 5 years, or for a shorter period if agreed upon by the partners, disbanding the partnership will be much less painful than if you have a 15-year sunset clause, which could prove untenable.

Once all the partners have agreed to the terms in the contract, the Articles of Partnership should be signed and dated by each partner.

Statistics on Partnerships

The IRS provides key data on partnerships in the United States in the quarterly IRS *Statistics of Income (SOI) Bulletins*, as summarized in

Table 3.2. These data reflect activities of all kinds of partnerships in the United States, including general partnerships, limited partnerships, joint ventures, and more.

Table 3.2 Statistics on partnerships

Number of Entities	3,763,117
Receipts (USD)	$7 trillion
Net Income (USD)	$792 billion

Source: U.S. Internal Revenue Service. 2019. *SOI Bulletins: Summer 2019.*

The total number of partnerships registered in the United States as of 2019 was 3.8 million, 85 percent fewer than the 25.5 million registered sole proprietorships. Despite the smaller number of partnerships, the $7 trillion in annual receipts into partnerships was five times larger than receipts for sole proprietorships. How can this be? There are fewer partnerships, yet these partnerships bring in far more money than sole proprietorships. Think back on our discussion of the types of industries where we tend to see businesses incorporated as partnerships: medical doctors, accountants, lawyers, financial firms. All of these professionals tend to charge relatively high professional fees for services that are captured in the higher receipts figures. After everyone is paid, partnerships netted $792 billion in 2019, more than twice the net income of sole proprietorships.

Why Start Your Business as a Partnership?

Why do businesspeople set up their businesses as partnerships? What are some of the advantages compared to sole proprietorships? Like sole proprietorships, partnerships are easy to start. One of the main considerations with a partnership is the time that must initially be devoted to seeking consensus among the partners as to what needs to be included in the all-important Articles of Partnership. There may be extra costs associated with consulting an attorney at law to be sure your contract meets the specific needs of your industry and partners.

Another advantage of a partnership is the ability to **pool resources** to establish, run, and grow your business. Think about what each partner could bring to your joint endeavor: prior experience in the industry or perhaps knowledge of one or more of the functional areas of business (e.g., finance, accounting, data science, supply-chain operations, advertising, public relations and/or management). Partnerships also enable you to pool finances to get your business going.

In addition to pooling resources, partnerships are synonymous with **shared accountability**. No longer are you working on your own. You have partners with whom you may consult before making decisions. And no matter how things turn out, all of the partners have a stake in the outcomes.

One final benefit is that partnerships do not have to pay corporate income taxes because they are pass-through entities. Like sole proprietors, partners are allowed to report to the IRS their share of the business's income, expenses, profits, and losses directly on the personal income tax form (IRS Form 1040). This reporting mechanism will save the partners' time, effort, and money.

Downsides of General Partnerships

It is important to note that every one of the general partners in your business has 100 percent responsibility for what happens in the partnership. As we discussed when analyzing sole proprietorships, this concept is known as **unlimited liability**, meaning that everything related to the business is the responsibility of the individual partners. Articles of Partnership do not protect owners from personal liability for debts and harms caused by their business partnerships.

Unlimited liability is tricky in partnerships because it means that you are responsible for any business-related activities and decisions made by your partners, even if the partners did not inform you of their actions ahead of time. The lesson here is to know your partners well and only go into business with individuals who share your notion of honesty and ethical practices, because the actions of one partner have ramifications for all the other partners—definitely a downside of this form of business entity. Please note that the concept of unlimited liability differs somewhat in the case of a limited partnership, discussed at the end of this chapter, whereby only one general partner holds unlimited liability, and the rest of the partners hold limited liability.

Valuable to note is that if a person has considerably more assets than the other potential partners, that person might consider the risks of becoming a partner. Under the law, a claimant may pursue a legal obligation such as a civil judgment against one partner or any number of partners. Therefore, it stands to reason that a person who wins a civil judgment against a partnership would pursue their financial award against the partner who has the deepest financial pockets.

To mitigate against surprises by your business partners, some people decide to open their partnerships with family members whom they know well. A case in point is the partnership established in 1963 by brothers Stanley and Sidney Goldstein, who opened a storefront that sold health and beauty products in Lowell, Massachusetts. The name of their business was **C**onsumer **V**alue **S**tores, which was later sold and became the nation's largest pharmacy—known simply as CVS—with a remarkable $195 billion in revenues in 2018.

Lastly, given that you are working side-by-side with other people who share ownership of this partnership, there may be **managerial disagreements** that can be arduous to handle. If you own your own business, you do not have to consult partners on how you might engage in the ongoing process of coordinating resources to reach your stated goals, the definition of management. Hence, management conforms to your style. Not so with partnerships, where it quickly becomes clear that owners may have different notions of how to oversee operations and make decisions.

Type 3: Corporations

In the United States, 2019 marked 200 years since a seminal moment occurred in the creation of a third type of business: the corporation.

In 1819, the U.S. Supreme Court handed down a ruling on an important case, *Trustees of Dartmouth College v. Woodward*, with the opinion written by Chief Justice John Marshall. As noted in the ruling, the Supreme Court gave extraordinary privileges to businesses holding private charters, allowing them to conduct business in a given state. Up to this point, private business charters were subject to state government oversight. But in 1819, the Supreme Court challenged state sovereignty over private corporate charters.

The Supreme Court did not regard the corporation as a type of citizen as was the case with sole proprietorships and partnerships, but rather as an *artificial entity* independent of the state. This legal case reflected the tensions in America at the time regarding what entity had the right to amend or repeal a corporate charter of a private commercial enterprise. The ruling deemed that corporate charters were not subject to changes by the state in which they were chartered, a ruling that was challenged for many decades yet prevailed and ultimately granted ever more autonomy to corporations.

How did the advent of this third type of business change commerce in the United States? The ruling established a new unit of analysis—the private corporation independent of state sovereignty—with rights that differed from sole proprietorships and partnerships. For example, a corporation could start a business and operate a business, as distinct from you (as an individual citizen) starting and operating a business. A corporation could buy and sell land, as distinct from individual citizens putting their names on land deeds. A corporation had the right to sue other entities (and persons) and be sued as well. A corporation could buy stock in another corporation. A corporation could enter into binding contracts.

All this may sound like no big deal. However, in the early nineteenth century, it was a big deal! The Supreme Court ruling fundamentally challenged the historical notion of business and determined that private corporate charters were "inviolate" and hence not subject to changes by state governments. It took some industrial magnates a long time to trust the new view on corporations, including steel magnate Andrew Carnegie, who consolidated his enormous business holdings into the Carnegie Steel Corporations in 1889 as a limited liability partnership to ensure his full control and ownership rights.

Over time, the notion of a third type of business, the private corporation, also known as a regular or C corporation, propelled the United

States toward becoming a nation in which commerce was increasingly conducted by privately chartered corporations within our capitalist economic system.

Statistics on Corporations

Table 3.3 presents statistics on corporations, drawing from the IRS *Statistics of Income Bulletins* through 2018. There are now almost 5.9 million corporations in the United States, far fewer than the 25.5 million sole proprietorships and only a bit more than the 3.8 million partnerships.

Table 3.3 Statistics on Corporations

Number of Entities	5,868,849
Receipts (USD)	$24.2 trillion
Net Income (USD)	$2 trillion

Source: U.S. Internal Revenue Service. 2019. *SOI Bulletins: Summer 2019.*

A different story emerges when we look at the dollars. In terms of all the money that comes into the various business entities, the IRS reports that corporate receipts last year reached $24.2 trillion! That means that the dollar value of all receipts coming into corporations was larger than the entire $20-trillion U.S. economy that same year. How much of these receipts did corporations get to keep? After every party that is owned money was paid, corporations kept $2 trillion in net income, a sizable profit that dwarfs those of partnerships and sole proprietorships.

Why Start Your Business as a Corporation?

The establishment of the corporation enabled businesspeople to grow their enterprises in ways not possible through structures such as sole proprietorship or partnerships in a burgeoning economy. What is it about corporations that distinguish them from other business types?

One factor is that corporations have access to more financial capital to establish and grow. For example, corporations have the right to sell stock in their firms as a means of raising equity capital. The idea of selling stock is to get other businesses, institutions, and individuals to give your business money in exchange for stock in the business.

Another key characteristic of the corporation is the notion that the owners do not have 100 percent responsibility for the activities of the business as is the case for sole proprietors and general partners who have unlimited liability. Rather, owners of a corporation and their representatives have what lawyers refer to as **limited liability**. In essence, corporations create a firewall between the owners and the corporation itself. If there is a problem with the business, the owners may not personally be sued in a civil lawsuit unless the owner has committed fraud in relation to business activities. By law, the corporation is treated as a legal person, separate from its founders, owners, the owner's representatives (e.g., executives and managers), and shareholders. Therefore, any aggrieved party must sue the corporation directly.

Similarly, if the business falls into debt, a creditor (or creditors) owed money must sue the corporation to make a claim on business assets instead of trying to secure payment through the owners' personal assets. Hence, corporate owners and their representatives are not at risk of losing their home or any other personal property in the event that a customer, creditor, or other agent is unhappy with what happens in the name of the corporation.

Another characteristic of a corporation is that the business will outlive the founders, owners, and their agents. The legal term is **perpetual life**. In contrast, if one of the co-owners in a general partnership dies, the business may or may not survive, depending on the terms specified in the Articles of Partnership.

Because corporations are endowed with the characteristics of personhood, another advantage of starting your business using this structure is the lawful ability of your corporation to lobby politicians and engage in electioneering, that is, the promotion of individual candidates for public office at the national, state, and municipal levels.

Downsides of Corporations

Starting a corporation is more difficult than starting either a partnership or sole proprietorship. Extra time and expense are required given the special laws and regulations pertaining to corporations. Hence, I recommend that if you decide to incorporate your business, consult an attorney to either handle such matters or help guide you through the process.

While corporations may remain small, most capitalize on the many advantages of the corporate form of organization to grow in size and scope over time, with its attendant challenges from a managerial perspective. In stark contrast to sole proprietorships, which can be run by a single individual, it is rare that a corporation can be run by a sole owner. Most corporations are staffed with employees who assume responsibility for each of the functional areas of business required to grow and be successful. Thus, the owners may not know all that is going on in a corporation, thus introducing challenges and problems that may be met with inflexibility due to size. In general, decision making takes longer in corporations compared to smaller entities.

Also viewed as a disadvantage when setting up your business as a corporation is the necessity to pay corporate income taxes on moneys earned, net of tax-deductible business expenses. C corporations must complete IRS Form 1120, the U.S. Corporation Income Tax Form, listing all income and expenditures. If the net income is non-negative, the corporation must pay corporate income tax according to guidelines provided by the IRS.

Trends in Business Types

We close this chapter with some notes on trends in business structure, beginning with a comparative analysis across business structures and closing with an examination of special-purpose business types such as the S corporation, Limited Partnership, and the Limited Liability Company.

The IRS *SOI Bulletins* data allow us to create a picture of all the businesses in the United States today and contrast the relative sizes of sole proprietorships, partnerships, and corporations using data filings with the IRS to 2019.

The IRS reported that a total of **35.2 million** businesses had the legal right to conduct business as corporations, partnerships, or sole proprietorships in the United States in 2019. To put that number in context, there is one business entity for every 11 people in the United States, which highlights the staggering amount of business activity in the country.

Out of these 35.2 million entities, a full 72 percent are sole proprietorships, underlining the general notion that small business is the backbone of America. Eleven percent of business entities are partnerships (of all kinds) and 17 percent are corporations.

With regard to business receipts in 2019, the IRS reports that total receipts for all business entities were $32.6 trillion. Only 4 percent of receipts were earned by sole proprietorships, 22 percent by partnerships, and 74 percent by corporations, signifying the volume of business transactions occurring within private corporations (Figure 3.1).

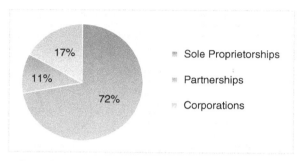

Figure 3.1 U.S. business entities by type: Percentage distribution
Source: U.S. Internal Revenue Service. 2019. *Statistics of Income Bulletins.*

Lastly, after all parties have been paid, including the IRS, $3.1 trillion remained as net income. Some 11 percent of net income went to sole proprietors, 25 percent to partnerships, and the remaining 64 percent to corporations.

Limited Partnership

Changes in statistical data provided by the IRS since the onset of the Great Recession in 2008 reveal that fewer businesspeople are setting up their enterprises as corporations. In contrast, the number of businesses registered as partnerships has risen, along with their receipts and net income earned.

Of particular interest is a rise in the formation of a particular kind of partnership known as a **Limited Partnership** (LP) since the beginning of the Wall Street financial crisis in 2007 and through the ensuing Great Recession. LPs are unique entities that in essence are a hybrid of the general partnership and the C corporation described earlier in this chapter.

Part Partnership: The LP hybrid leverages the unique advantages of partnerships and corporations to create a robust new entity. Limited partnerships have the advantage of being smaller than most corporations, thus limiting the number of owners and providing a freer hand in managing the business. LPs are taxed like a partnership and hence pay no corporate income tax. LPs also have less public reporting, which saves time, energy, and money.

Part Corporation: At the same time, LPs are similar to corporations in that almost all of the business partners carry limited liability. By law, only one of the owners in an LP must hold unlimited liability and pay self-employment taxes toward Medicare and Social Security. The notion of perpetual life also applies to LPs, like corporations, and LPs may raise money by issuing publicly tradable shares of stock, thus facilitating the securing of equity finance.

S Corporation

The other kind of corporation that exhibits traits of both partnerships and corporations is the **S corporation** under Subchapter 5 of the IRS code. The IRS established this kind of corporation in the post–World War II era, when the country was encouraging the creation of small Mom & Pop Shops. S corporations do not pay corporate income taxes; rather, owners report profits and losses on the IRS Form 1040 personal income tax form. All owners carry limited liability.

Constraints on S corporations include a limit of 100 allowable shareholders and a requirement that all shareholders be U.S. citizens or legal residents. Some states do not recognize the S corporation business structure and/or may put in place a cap on the total receipts such entities may earn, above which the business will be treated as a standard C corporation.

Limited Liability Company

The other type of corporation growing in popularity today is the **Limited Liability Company (LLC)**. In addition to members benefiting from personal limited liability protection, LLCs may choose how it will be taxed. If there are two or more partners, it may elect to be taxed like a

partnership. If there is only one owner, it may be taxed as a sole proprietorship. The LLC has the option of being taxed as a regular C corporation or an S corporation.

The LLC is another example of a hybrid business entity emulating
certain characteristics of corporations, partnerships, and sole proprietorships. LLC owners are called members who are protected against personal
liability for all business activities, obligations, and debts. The members
record profits and losses directly on their IRS Form 1040 as personal
income that is not taxed as corporate earnings. Hence, financial activities
pass through the LLC directly to the owner.

Of interest to the IRS is the recent use of the LLC business structure
for philanthropic and lobbying activities. Some wealthy Americans are
using the LLC private business structure to manage their philanthropic
activities, including donations. Over the past 100 years, wealthy businesspeople who gave away large portions of their wealth established private
foundations. Per IRS guidelines, these entities are granted 501(c)(3) status as tax-exempt entities, meaning money donated to the private foundation could be deducted from the donor's personal income taxes. In return,
private foundations are required to distribute at least 5 percent of the
foundation's assets each year for charitable purposes, disclose the recipients of foundation grants, and not engage in lobbying or electioneering,
according to the Tax Reform Act of 1969.

Facebook founder Mark Zuckerberg has opted to use the Limited Liability Company mechanism to manage his and his wife's (Priscilla Chan)
philanthropic endeavors. By funneling 99 percent of the couple's Facebook shares (valued at $45 billion) through an LLC, named the Chan
Zuckerberg Initiative, Chan and Zuckerberg (a) retain control over how
their money is invested or donated, (b) skirt the 5 percent private foundation payout requirements (which would require a $2.25 billion dis-
tribution each year on $45 billion of assets), (c) retain rights to lobby
for political causes, (d) avoid public disclosure of what is done with the
money in the LLC, and (e) may invest the money in their LLC not only
in nonprofit entities but also for-profit business interests in the United
States and abroad.

Zuckerberg and Chan join the ranks of others who have channeled
philanthropic ventures through an LLC. Zuckerberg's announcement on

December 1, 2015, that he and his wife will transfer the equivalent of $45 billion in Facebook stock to a LLC reflected a savvy business financial transaction based on keen knowledge of the legal factors governing business structures in the United States today, something every successful businessperson would benefit from understanding.

Wrap Up

When starting a new business, do not be too concerned about choosing just the right type of structure to meet your business vision. However, knowing from the start the distinction between sole proprietorships, partnerships, and corporations will leave you with a better sense of the advantages and disadvantages of each type of legal structure. U.S. law is such that you may change your business type if you deem it valuable over time, another reason we like to conduct business in the United States!

CHAPTER 4

Growth

Thus far, we have defined what a business is, considered different types of business structures with an eye toward helping you select the business model that suits your interests, and considered how your business fits into the $20 trillion U.S. economy, with its business cycle fluctuations and 35.2 million enterprises competing with one another.

Next, we will explore ways that you can grow your business through the production of goods and services, another piece of our definition of business.

What Is a Business?

An organization
comprised of people
who produce goods and services
to sell
to earn a profit
distributed to stakeholders

For most businesses, the ultimate aim is to grow in size and scope in order to increase revenues and ultimately profits. Toward this aim, you have some choices to make. One avenue to pursue is finding ways to grow your business while staying in the United States, which is the focus of this chapter. Another avenue is to grow your business by going global, to be explored in the next chapter. We will examine both domestic and global avenues so that you come away with a full set of options to consider when the time is right.

While some students are eager to go global, others do not have the urge to travel and/or run a business that requires engaging in commerce with business-people in other countries. There is no right or wrong here. The choice is yours.

And if you decide to stay local, there are many ways that enable you to expand your business by doing what is familiar in your own country.

Option #1: Domestic Growth from Within

Some businesspeople employ the strategy called *growth from within* to expand operations domestically. Imagine a scenario whereby you have started your own business, which is doing well. You have a loyal customer base, you produce products (or services) that are in demand, and you are making more in revenues than you expend in costs and, hence, are earning a profit. You are proud of your success and ready for more.

A *growth from within* strategy would entail doing more of what you already know works well for you and your customers. You might consider, for instance, producing a different type of product at an existing manufacturing facility. You might consider expanding your customer base by reaching out to a different age group. You might explore setting up a new production or sales base in a different location. In other words, continue what your business is already doing well but on a larger scale or scope.

To my mind, the *growth from within* strategy has been used very effectively at my university, Mount St. Mary's. Established in 1808 as Mount St. Mary's College, it is the second oldest Catholic institution of higher education in the United States, second to Georgetown University in Washington, DC. For more than a century and a half, the Mount educated young men seeking baccalaureate and seminarian degrees.

In 1972, the Mount made a significant strategic decision to grow from within by allowing the all-male college to start admitting women. Overnight, the Mount's customer base doubled, a winning strategy, as almost 60 percent of the student body attending colleges in the United States today is female.

This strategy was met with ease from a logistical perspective given that the university had a history of offering degree programs on a beautiful campus with capable professors, staff, and administrators who delivered accredited baccalaureate programs. The Mount's core business model remained the same, with the only logistical difference being the need to build and operate a women's dormitory to accommodate the new female student body. Today 56 percent of Mount students are female, making this a successful business strategy.

Another growth spurt at the Mount began in 2006 when the Board of Trustees sought to elevate Mount St. Mary's College to university status, hence offering masters-level courses, programs, and degrees. With state approval in 2009, the institution was renamed Mount St. Mary's University and established the School of Business, School of Liberal Arts, School of Science and Mathematics, and School of Education, each of which offers graduate degrees. Today, more than 10 percent of Mount students are conducting graduate studies, another success story.

Option #2: Domestic Licensing

While there are many advantages to starting and running your business as a sole proprietor, you will quickly find that there is a limit to how much money you can earn.

> While there are many advantages to starting and running your business as a sole proprietor, you will quickly find that there is a limit to how much money you can earn.

If you own a Certified Public Accounting (CPA) firm, for example, there is a cap on the number of billable hours in a given week. The same holds true for teachers, researchers, excavators, carpenters, lawyers, physical therapists, or plumbers established as sole proprietorships, whose earnings are constrained not by skill or knowledge but by time.

One way that you can grow your business while retaining sole ownership is through licensing your business model to capable service providers interested in what you do for a living. This is a very popular model among yoga teachers today. After years of training as yogis and running their own studios, yoga teachers are growing their businesses by setting up trademarked yoga-teaching training schools that grant students the right

PLANK

to teach yoga under a proprietary brand name or trademark.

This is a form of licensing whereby the yoga teacher (and business owner) works with people who are interested in becoming licensed yoga instructors. The owner shares her knowledge and experience accumulated running a yoga studio. The students pay to train with the yogi for a set number of contact hours (200, 300, 500), after which the student receives a diploma, indicating she is fit to teach yoga. Some yogi business owners go one step further and franchise their yoga studios to students who have gone through the owner's formal yoga teacher training programs.

The trick with this model, however, is to include a noncompete agreement that limits your students' ability to set up yoga studios in the vicinity of your studio. Geographic noncompete clauses date back to the guilds in fifteenth- and sixteenth-century Western Europe, where young apprentices were barred from opening a shop within the same town as their mentors to avoid the possibility of stealing customers. This is where the term "journeymen" first appeared, meaning once you received your training, you had to journey down the road so you could not compete with your mentor.

Option #3: Domestic Mergers and Acquisitions

Another example of how to grow your business domestically is via a merger and acquisition in the same country in which you operate.

Mergers and acquisitions, commonly referred to as M&As, enable businesses to consolidate operations in order to grow. Mergers are voluntary consolidations between two businesses eager to become one new entity, such as when the oil giant Exxon paid $79 billion to purchase Mobil Oil in 1998 and became ExxonMobil. An acquisition may be a targeted and/or hostile takeover of one business by another with the intention of doing away with the competition and dominating an industry. If both business entities involved in the M&A are registered to do business in the same country, this is considered a domestic growth strategy.

The number and type of M&As change over time. Historically, the United States experienced M&A peaks during the 1890s, the 1920s, 1960s, late 1980s, 1990s, and mid-2010s. Various precipitating events may trigger an increase in M&A activities, for example, economic shocks like the explosive growth in personal computers and usage in the 1990s. Mergers also may be triggered by a quick drop in aggregate demand among buyers in an industry, leaving excess capacity ripe for acquisition. Significant changes in the regulatory environment may lead to mergers, as well as changes in financial conditions such as the build-up of large amounts of cash on the balance sheets of digital platform firms in the mid-2010s that led to the buyout of many smaller digital firms that held the promise of becoming serious competitors to giant firms.

From a business perspective, a merger or acquisition is a form of investment. There are three major kinds of M&As, each of which serves a unique business purpose.

Horizontal M&As

Horizontal mergers and acquisitions entail the purchase of one business by another business engaged in the same industry or line of operation, for example, one shoe manufacturer buying another shoe manufacturer. The result of horizontal integration is to limit the competition within a particular industry.

Cellular carriers made the news from 2017 to 2019 with talk of a possible merger between the Sprint Corporation (valued at $28 billion) and T-Mobile US Inc. (valued at $52 billion). When measured by the number of mobile subscribers, Sprint is the third-largest carrier in the United States, followed by T-Mobile. Combining operations would result in a single carrier with 126 million subscribers. Merger talks were of great interest to competitors Verizon Wireless and AT&T Inc., which currently dominate the U.S. telecommunications industry.

If the merger were to succeed, the plan would be

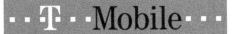

to allow the chief executive officer of T-Mobile US Inc. to become the chief executive of the combined enterprise and for Sprint's chairperson to oversee the newly formed board of directors. On November 4, 2017, Sprint and T-Mobile issued a joint statement calling off the merger, citing an inability to find common ground—but not before the firms created a new logo imagining a possible Sprint and T-Mobile merger in the future. Indeed, 5 months later, the two firms began renewed merger talks, the third time since 2014. In April 2019, the U.S. Department of Justice issued a preliminary ruling indicating that the proposed $26 billion merger was unlikely to be approved because it is a threat to competition. Reversing course, the U.S. Department of Justice approved the merger in July 2019. Stay tuned!

In an effort to upscale its image, Walmart is also aggressively engaging in horizontal M&As by purchasing small niche online clothing boutiques, such as Bonobos in 2017 for $310 million. The year prior, Walmart purchased ShoeBuy, Moosejaw.com, ModCloth.com, and Jet. com (for $3.3 billion), signaling an effort to move beyond a no-frills image, attract more affluent urban shoppers, and push up its prices.[1] Horizontal M&As may help Walmart expand its customer base in the increasingly competitive retail industry that is challenging Walmart's status as the world's largest retailer.

Vertical M&As

In contrast to a horizontal merger, a **vertical merger or acquisition** entails a firm buying a business that is part of its supply chain rather than a direct competitor. The objective is for the acquiring business to exercise more control over its supply chain in the hopes of increasing profits.

A much-talked-about possible vertical merger that has been in the works since 2017 is between the oldest health insurer in the country, Aetna ($63 billion revenues), and the largest U.S. pharmacy, CVS Health

---

[1] A. Bhattarai. May 25, 2018. "Does Walmart Take the Shine off Its High-End Acquisitions?" *Seattle Times,* https://snewsi.com/id/18273629197.

($177 billion revenues). The merger would bring together three key layers of the health industry supply chain:

1. retail pharmacies that fill prescriptions (e.g., CVS with 23 percent of all pharmacy revenues in the United States);
2. pharmacy benefits managers (PBM), intermediaries that negotiate drug prices for medical plans (of which CVS is the largest, managing 24 percent of all PBM claims for clients such as Aetna); and
3. health-care insurers (e.g., Aetna, which represents 6 percent of the U.S. health insurance industry).

The U.S. Department of Justice approved the CVS Health and Aetna $69 billion merger on October 10, 2018. CVS moved aggressively to seek approval of the buyout in order to drive Aetna's 22-million health insurance enrollees to CVS Health's 9,700 pharmacies and 1,000 Minute Clinics. The urgency of the $69-billion offer was fueled by speculation that e-commerce giant Amazon.com Inc. would soon acquire more pharmacies, build pharmacies into its newly purchased Whole Foods Market grocery stores, and expand its mail order and delivery prescription drug model, the latter signaled by its June 2018 purchase of the online pharmacy business, PillPack, for an estimated $1 billion.

Because the U.S. Department of Justice concerns itself primarily with horizontal mergers when enforcing antitrust laws, it approved the CVS–Aetna merger, which it viewed as a vertical M&A rather than a horizontal M&A. The CVS–Aetna deal might well become a template for other vertical mergers in not only the health industry but also other industries. For example, Tesla is known for being a vertically integrated business as it produces some 80 percent of its electric vehicles, sells them directly to customers, owns and operates a network of service stations across the United States, opened the world's largest lithium-ion battery factory in Nevada, and built a highway that connects the factory to the Silver Peak Mine, the only lithium-ion mine in the United States.

Vertical M&As have an historical precedent in the United States, dating back to the captains of industry during the Gilded Age (late 1870s to 1900). John D. Rockefeller, for example, set up Standard Oil as a vertically integrated business by acquiring as many elements as he could in the oil supply chain, from land and oil wells to refineries and delivery wagons. Henry Ford did the same when founding the Ford Motor Company on the belief that "If you want it done right, do it yourself."[2]

Despite the long-term success of vertical integration, U.S. businesses steered away from this model in the 1980s in favor of subcontracting out pieces of their supply chains to reduce costs and retain only core business elements.

Forty years later, firms are returning to the practices of the turn-of-the-twentieth-century industrialists, arguing that doing things in-house is more efficient and quicker than contracting out pieces of the supply chain. Thus, we see Netflix and Amazon creating their own content for television shows and movies viewed by customers who might otherwise seek content from competitors on cable or network television. The benefits of vertical integration propelled Costa Cruises and Walt Disney to purchase Caribbean islands to ensure a pleasant experience for sea-faring customers and avoid geopolitical uncertainties impacting their growing businesses.

Perhaps we will continue to see renewed interest in vertical mergers and acquisitions, such as the CVS Health–Aetna proposed merger.

Conglomerate M&As

In addition to vertical and horizontal M&As, there are **conglomerate mergers and acquisitions**, whereby the parties involved in negotiations are neither direct competitors nor part of each other's supply chain. Rather than specialize in a single industry (e.g., banking, automobiles, retail trade, steel, software), businesses are branching out to establish themselves as conglomerates that produce, service, and/or sell products that reach across an array of industries, products, and services.

The formation of conglomerates was a popular strategy in the twentieth century, when internationally minded corporations vastly diversified portfolios by purchasing nonrelated businesses with the aim of rapid

---

[2]H. Ford. 1926. *Today and Tomorrow* (New York, NY: Productivity Press).

growth and expansion across the globe. Such was the case when Andrew Carnegie sold his famed Carnegie Steel Company to financier J.P. Morgan in 1901, reflecting the banker's diversified portfolio strategy. On July 8, 1986, J.P. Morgan renamed its U.S. Steel division to simply U.S.X. to reflect the firm's further diversification well beyond steel.

The historical roots in diversification through conglomerate M&As appeared to be back in vogue in the 2010s. Growing interest in conglomerates is now a global phenomenon. In fact, business conglomerates represent some 70 percent of business enterprises in Asia and 60 percent of the listed enterprises on India's stock exchanges.

Amazon.com Inc. provides the most visible, large-scale illustration of a conglomerate in the United States today. Established  in 1996 as an online book store, Amazon grew, as envisioned by founder Jeff Bezos, into an empire that includes physical book stores; online retail sales of all types of goods and services; drone manufacturers; autonomous humanoid robotic research; military contracting; the newspaper business, with his purchase of *The Washington Post*; and, most recently, retail grocery stores, with its 2017 buy-out of Whole Foods Market (for $13.7 billion), one of the largest organic food chains in the United States. Bezos continues to experiment with growth strategies to great acclaim with $4 out of every $10 spent online in the United States going to the digital platform giant.

Parallel Entrepreneurs

In frontier economies, where there is rapid growth and a burgeoning consumer middle class, we are seeing a spin-off of conglomerates, referred to as *parallel entrepreneurs*, emerging. Parallel entrepreneurship refers to businesspeople who create, own, and run a network of several different business entities across an array of industries within one country. These entities are not conglomerates run by one firm; nor are they set up to be potentially merged with or acquired by another business. Rather, the owner sees a benefit in owning several distinct legal entities engaged in different activities.

Africa is a case in point. Why? Some entrepreneurs are capitalizing on the wealth of business opportunities in countries such as Ghana, Nigeria, and Kenya, where entrepreneurs own, on average, six businesses each.[3] Parallel entrepreneurs report that once they have established a high level of trust among customers, it is easy to introduce another service to the same customers, especially in businesses that are relationship-based (e.g., management consulting, finance, and internet service providers). Parallel entrepreneurs also indicate that at times it may be easier to raise small amounts of money for each business rather than raise a large sum for a single entity. In addition, African businesspeople often face unpredictability vis-à-vis national policies, laws, and government officials that deters them from putting all their money into a single business. In these cases, a diversified set of business interests may be advantageous.

The venerable Tata family business, founded in 1868 in India by Jamsetji Tata, known as the **Tata Group**, represents one of the largest parallel entrepreneurships in the world, with 100 divisions and 28 publicly-listed enterprise in 2018. The family business strategy extended operations well beyond its key revenue-makers: steel, motor vehicles, power, telecoms, information technology, and hotels to now include salt, Tata Global Beverages, chemicals, transportation, Tata Consulting Services, Tata Asset Management, Tata Management and Training Centre, Taj Hotels Resorts and Palaces, and next defense, infrastructure, and finance.

Since 2012, Cyrus Mistry has chaired the Tata Group. He is only the sixth chair of the 150-year-old firm and the first boss from outside the Tata family, taking over from the world-renown Ratan Tata, who oversaw an increase in his family firm's revenues from $6 billion to $100 billion between 1991 and 2012 to create a global workforce of about 700,000 people in over 80 countries.[4] Tata Sons, the parent company of this empire, is not listed on a stock exchange, leaving business decisions still under the control of the founding family.[5]

Tata represents a new kind of highly diversified, global transnational corporate enterprise on the rise in frontier economies across the globe, challenging traditional Western business structures and growth strategies.

[3]The Economist. June 23, 2012. "African Entrepreneurs: Parallel Players," p. 69.
[4]The Economist. March 5, 2011. "The Tata Group: Out of India," pp. 75–77.
[5]The Economist. September 24, 2016. "Tata Group: Mistry's Elephant," p. 23.

Option #4: Breaking Up a Business

One other way to grow your business is quite the opposite of a merger and acquisition. It is possible for a firm to realize that, in order to grow, it may be advantageous to break up the firm into separate businesses. Such was the case in January 2018 when John Flannery, CEO of General Electric, announced that the conglomerate was considering selling divisions worth $20 billion (out of $365 billion in total assets) and restructuring GE into three core operations: energy, aviation, and health insurance.[6]

This sell-off is an attempt to rid GE of nonperforming assets such as GE Capital's life and health-insurance portfolios and to reverse the 40 percent share price decline in 2017. Despite this strategic effort, in June of 2018, the Dow Jones Industrial Average removed General Electric from its 30-firm index despite GE having been one of the Dow's original components in 1986. General Electric's spot was filled by the new Walgreens Boots pharmacy chain.

Option #5: Shoot-Outs

Businesspeople continue to find interesting and effective ways to grow their businesses. Some strategies are new versions of existing growth models; others are altogether novel approaches.

Digital media firms in particular are engaging in such a new approach. An online digital platform provides a place where buyers and sellers come together to exchange products, a similar concept to stock exchanges and retail malls. Digital platforms are growing in size and are dominated by a handful of businesses, notably Facebook, Alphabet's Google, and Amazon. Today, digital firms that own and operate online platforms are engaging in nonconventional mergers and acquisitions called shoot-outs, in which they buy a smaller business that has yet to show positive net revenues, yet is viewed as a potential rival.

The Parliament in London, England, reported that in 2016, Google (owned by parent company Alphabet) purchased 187 tech firms viewed as potential competitors.[7] This came on the heels of Facebook's announcement

---

[6]The Economist. January 20, 2018. "Business," p. 9.
[7]The Economist. May 28, 2016. "Online Platforms: Nostrums for Rostrums," p. 111.

on February 19, 2014, that it paid $19 billion to buy a small firm called WhatsApp, known for its message app that sends messages over mobile broadband. While shoot-out acquisitions squelch competition among small businesses, they help large digital platforms grow, creating a quandary in a winner-take-all economic environment where fierce competition exists among the largest firms.

Wrap Up

Whether you are in a highly competitive industry or one with low competition, there are a host of ways that you can grow your business in addition to the options presented in this chapter. Read on to explore further growth options by going global.

CHAPTER 5

Going Global

Today, studying business is unlike anything we have seen before. One difference is how we differentiate between the study of business and the study of global business. The study of business is now the study of global business—there is no distinction.

> Today, the study of business is the study of global business—there is no distinction.

If we study mergers and acquisitions, for example, we can apply what we learn to businesses in any country around the world. If we study finance, we can apply what we learn to global arbitrage and finance across the globe. If we determine that marketing and public relations is our favorite functional area, we can apply what we learn in any location.

Our world is incredibly intertwined. There are 195 countries on planet Earth, of which 193 are member states of the United Nations, with the remaining two being nonmember observer states: The Vatican and the State of Palestine. Politicians and diplomats work diligently to engage with businesspeople the world over in dynamic ways. Cultures vary incredibly from country to country. Languages are rich and varied throughout the world, where some 5,000 languages are spoken. Electronics enable us to communicate globally every day, 24 hours a day. Global business supply chains have become even more expansive as there are fewer barriers to interconnectedness. Jobs in business can take us anywhere on the planet, as my career demonstrates, and I hope yours will too.

 It is a very exciting time to study business—global business—because global capitalism reaches almost every corner of our planet in the twenty-first century. It is fascinating to figure out how your business might be able to expand globally or at least connect with businesses, financiers, and consumers in other countries. Thanks to global capitalism, this is all very real and possible for you today.

Global Capitalism

What do I mean when using the term "global capitalism"? In a nutshell, global capitalism encapsulates the following:

Global capitalism is an economic framework to understand how society chooses to organize itself to meet economic, social, and financial needs.
Global capitalism promotes competition in one single world economy.
Global capitalism enables material, human, and financial resources to flow freely around planet earth.
Global capitalism creates a structure and process by which businesses can expand globally.

To paint a picture of global capitalism, consider salient statistics from 2018 to 2019 that capture the imagination and boggle the mind:

- Transnational trade flows are valued at $20 trillion;
- Global GDP is estimated to be $80 trillion;
- 244 million international migrants work worldwide (myself included);
- Official foreign exchange reserves total $11 trillion;
- $5 trillion in electronic currencies move around the planet daily; and
- Funds invested in derivatives totaled $1.2 quadrillion.

I am fascinated with the phenomenon called global capitalism that is sweeping the globe in full view and have made it my life's work to understand its nuances and how it impacts us from a business perspective.

Terminology

Our exploration into the world of business today can get complicated fairly quickly. Hence, our terminology has evolved. When I was in college, any reference to business outside the United States was referred to as **international** business or international commerce, building on the simple two-country trade model introduced by neoclassical economists in the nineteenth century. By the end of the twentieth century, global business had expanded well beyond the two-country trade model and required new terminology. Businesspeople settled on the term **multinational** to represent two or more nations conducting business together. Today, with finance, global arbitrage, big data, and global supply chains leading us toward a whole new understanding of global commerce, we often speak of **transnational** corporations (TNCs).

Transnational corporations exhibit the following characteristics:

1. TNCs are corporate legal entities as defined by respective governments;
2. TNCs conduct business across borders, whereby two or more nations are engaged;
3. TNCs tend to be large business entities; and
4. TNCs have no allegiance to any one country (or locality).

Think about how the world-renowned transnational corporation **Disney** produces its iconic films under global capitalism. The movie concept might be conceived in country A; the writers are in country B; the animation is done in country C; filming takes place in country D; Disney buys parts and supplies for filming from countries E, A, B, and C; the final product is sent to fulfillment centers in country G, and it is ultimately sold to viewers in countries A through Z.

The Largest TNCs

Let's take a look at the finances of some of the largest TNCs and explore the degree to which these entities are engaged in global capitalism from a financial perspective.

One method of analyzing the global connectedness of transnational corporations is by looking at the amount of cash businesses keep offshore, meaning not in the home country. According to Oxfam America in 2016, the 50 largest public companies registered in the United States held a total of $1.4 trillion offshore on global profits of $4.2 trillion.[1] The five largest of this group and the amounts kept offshore were as follows in 2016:

1.	Apple	$181 bn
2.	General Electric	$119 bn
3.	Microsoft	$108 bn
4.	Pfizer	$74 bn
5.	IBM	$61 bn

The following year—in 2017—the amount of cash held offshore by these same firms rose $200 billion to a total of $1.6 trillion.[2] The list is led by the following five firms:

1.	Apple	$200 bn
2.	Pfizer	$194 bn
3.	Microsoft	$124 bn
4.	General Electric	$104 bn
5.	IBM	$68 bn

A second measure of global connectedness is the percentage of assets TNCs invest in foreign countries. The United Nations' *World Investment Report* (2018) lists the biggest transnational corporations, excluding financial institutions, such as big banks and investment houses. According to the UN, Royal Dutch Shell had the greatest assets of all nonfinancial

---

[1]Oxfam America. April 14, 2016. *Broken at the Top.*
[2]Oxfam America. April 12, 2017. *Rigged Reform.*

businesses in 2016 equal to $411 billion. A reported 85 percent of the firm's assets were not in the home country of England, but rather were invested elsewhere across the globe. Does having only 15 percent of total assets invested in the home country mean that Royal Dutch Shell is not an English business? Consider the huge energy firm Total SA, incorporated in France. Out of its $244 billion in assets, some 96 percent were not invested in France in 2016. Does this mean Total SA is not a French firm?

The answer lies in your definition of a domestic versus global business. If assets are your metric, Table 5.1 might suggest how truly global the world of business has become in the twenty-first century.

Table 5.1 World's biggest nonfinancial TNCs

Ranked by Foreign Assets in 2016				
TNC (Home Country)	Sector	Foreign Assets	Total Assets	Percent Foreign Assets
Royal Dutch Shell (England)	Energy	$349.7 bn	$411.3 bn	85%
Toyota Motor Corp (Japan)	Motor Vehicles	$303.7 bn	$436.0 bn	70%
BP plc (England)	Energy	$235.1 bn	$263.3 bn	89%
Total SA (France)	Energy	$233.2 bn	$243.5 bn	96%
Anheuser-Busch InBev NV (Belgium)	Food & Beverages	$208.0 bn	$258.4 bn	81%

Source: United Nations Conference on Trade and Development. 2018. *World Investment Report.*

How You Can Go Global with Your Business

If you are ready to consider going global with your business, what are some of your options? Below are seven options to get you thinking. While not all-inclusive, perhaps when you are ready, you'll refer back to this list for ideas.

Option #1: Global Licensing

Suppose you own and run a manufacturing plant located in the United States that produces a line of clothing and accessories for sale domestically. For years you have wanted to expand your handbag line and have had your eye on **Louis Vuitton** products. What are your options? One idea is to approach Louis Vuitton in France and explore the possibility of establishing a business-to-business global licensing agreement.

Louis Vuitton is a world-renowned maker of purses, handbags, wallets, shoes, clothing, and luggage that dates back to 1854 when a man named Louis Vuitton started the business. Since his death, the firm has continued to grow and expand its product line. The firm may be interested in granting you a license to use its manufacturing techniques to produce its handbags in your U.S.-based manufacturing plant in return for a licensing fee.

Global licensing agreements are possible in an array of industries. In exchange for a licensing fee, the grantor of the license will provide what is needed for the foreign business to legally reproduce its products (e.g., recipes, patents, training, etc.). The Louis Vuitton purses you manufacture and sell would be sold as originals, not knock-offs, and bear a label that says, "Made in the USA." Most consumers would have no clue that your business is engaged in global commerce.

Global licensing allows you to take your business global without your having to leave the United States, which is an advantage for some businesspeople.

Option #2: Foreign Direct Investment

One of the downsides of Louis Vuitton granting global licensing agreements is the risk that the business that pays for a license does not reproduce the handbags according to Louis Vuitton's strict quality standards. If this persists, Louis Vuitton risks having its reputation impugned. So, let's consider a second option to go global to mitigate such risk.

Option #2 is what is known as foreign direct investment. In this case, for example, a U.S. business might consider investing in a business in another country that has a strong business model and potential for expansion. The U.S. firm does not buy out the entire business but rather makes an equity investment by buying a stake of at least 10 percent in the foreign business.

Conversely, a foreign business might be interested in investing money in a U.S. business through the foreign direct investment (FDI) vehicle. This kind of equity investing goes on all around the world and is tracked each year by the United Nations. In 2018, total foreign direct investment was estimated to be $1.3 trillion, with the largest source worldwide from the United States, followed by Japan and China. That sum, however, is lower than the $1.4 trillion in FDI reported for 2017, primarily due to less money flowing to developed countries.[3] The United Nations' *World Investment Report* shows in detail how FDI changes from year to year and lays out where the money comes from and where it is invested.

Why would a business directly invest money in a business in another country? The German automaker BMW invested in a research-and-development facility in Thailand to expand BMWs research facilities beyond what is possible in its Munich, Germany, facility. Given BMW's high standards for automotive design and manufacturing, BMW's FDI agreement gave the German firm hands-on control rights at the Thai facility. In contrast, other businesses invest equity in foreign firms as purely a financial transaction with no intention of managing or working directly with the foreign firm or even visiting the venture.

FDI is what is known as an equity mode of investing directly in another business. In contrast, a licensing agreement is a nonequity mode of going global. Both options allow you to go global without leaving the United States.

Option #3: Global Mergers and Acquisitions

Like domestic mergers and acquisitions, global M&As present a mechanism for businesses to work together, voluntarily or involuntarily. Usually, mergers are voluntary associations between the owners and agents of two businesses that would mutually benefit by becoming a single business entity. Involuntary associations, in contrast, are not necessarily an advantage for both parties. The asymmetry stems from one business taking over another by becoming the majority shareholder or dominant voice on the

---

[3]United Nations Conference on Trade and Development. 2019. *World Investment Report* (New York, NY: United Nations).

board of directors. Let's look at some recent M&As that involved businesses registered in two different countries.

Verizon Wireless

When merger talks began in 2013, Verizon Wireless, the largest mobile service carrier in the United States (est. 1999), was owned by two businesses. Verizon Communications, registered in the United States, owned 55 percent, and Vodafone, registered in England, owned 45 percent. With the aim of complete ownership and control of Verizon Wireless, on September 2, 2013, Verizon Communications announced a friendly buyout of all of Vodafone shares for $130 billion.

The Verizon Wireless buyout was the third largest business transaction in recorded history, preceded by the Vodafone Airtouch $198-billion takeover of Germany's Mannesmann and the AOL/Time Warner $165-billion merger, which both took place in 2000. The sheer size of these three M&As attests to the importance of the wireless communication industry under global capitalism today.

Chrysler

Chrysler, one of the three venerable automobile makers in the United States, went through tremendous upheaval in 2013 that resulted in Chrysler being bought out by Fiat, an Italian automobile maker. When takeover talks began, Chrysler was owned by two businesses: Fiat, with 58.5 percent ownership, and VEBA, a U.S.-based trade union health-care trust that owned 41.5 percent. Initially, Fiat announced its intention to increase its ownership of Chrysler to 75 percent but ultimately sought full ownership.

Chrysler is a famous car maker, whose history includes tremendous successes alongside tremendous failures, the latter of which required significant government financial bailouts in the 1980s and again during the Wall Street financial crisis in the late 2000s. In 2008, Chrysler declared bankruptcy and the U.S. government provided funds to bail out the business. While this provided a temporary stopgap measure to enable Chrysler to keep its doors open, the government is not in the business of owning and operating a car company. So, the Italian auto maker, Fiat, proposed to the U.S. government to buy a 20 percent stake in Chrysler, which was accepted. Gradually, Fiat's stake rose to 58.5 percent in 2013, at which point it announced the intention of a full buyout of Chrysler and approached the other owner of Chrysler, VEBA.

Fiat and VEBA came to the negotiating table and presented their respective valuations of VEBA's 41.5 percent share in Chrysler. Fiat's number was $1.8 billion; VEBA's number was $4.3 billion, quite a difference. People at both firms worked fast and furiously to reconcile the difference, and on January 1, 2014, announced that a deal had been made for Fiat to buy out all of VEBA's shares in Chrysler for $4.35 billion.

As a result, Chrysler is no longer a U.S. business, leaving only two major U.S. car companies, Ford and General Motors. Fiat has since moved its 115-year-old headquarters from Italy to the Netherlands. Its tax residence is England, and its stock is listed on the New York Stock Exchange. That's global capitalism!

This well-known global M&A illustrates the intricacies of doing business under global capitalism and the value of learning the nature of going global with your business.

Option #4: Global Manufacturing

Industries engaged in manufacturing products may also go global to grow the business. Take, for example, a factory located in the United States that produces automobiles.

If you wanted to take this business global, there are a couple of possibilities to consider. First, you would review where the inputs to producing the cars in your factory come from. It is possible that all the materials required to assemble a car are made in the United States, for example, steel, tires, aluminum, leather, nuts and bolts, and so on. If you have connections with suppliers of these inputs and are happy with their products, you may have no incentive to look elsewhere for suppliers. But if you want to consider other sources that may produce a better or a cheaper product, then global manufacturing may be preferable. In this case, you would travel the world interviewing businesses in foreign countries that produce the specific inputs needed for production. If an agreement is made, you would then import these products into the United States and transport them to your factory.

A second way to go global if you are a manufacturer is on the back end; meaning, after you have purchased all the necessary inputs to production and assembled the car, you may opt to sell not only to dealerships in the United States but also to dealerships in other countries. In this case, exporting the finished product is a way to go global and grow your business.

If this option intrigues you, studying supply chain operations and logistics is the next step. Such programs are being offered on more college campuses today, including my university, Mount St. Mary's. In 2011, the seven sons of Richard J. Bolte Sr. honored their father, who founded BDP International (est. 1966) in Philadelphia, Pennsylvania, with an endowment to name our school the Richard J. Bolte Sr. School of Business at Mount St. Mary's University. BDP International is now one of the world's largest logistics and transportation service firms, moving products across 120 countries (see https://www.bdpinternational.com/locations).

Option #5: Big Box Store

Another option to go global is the Big Box Store model, a phenomenon that is sweeping the world due to the remarkable capabilities of logistics firms like BDP International. Modern-day shipping and other transportation systems have enabled consumers to purchase goods manufactured across the planet at an affordable price. Commerce in the United States changed dramatically over the past century from being a system primarily driven by small entrepreneurs who owned and operated sole proprietorships catering to a local clientele. Today, transnational corporations dominate commerce and have created a system whereby place matters less and less.

Consider, for example, the creation of the world's largest retail chain, Walmart, started by Sam Walton in 1962, when he opened the first Walmart Discount City story in Rogers, Arkansas. His one-stop business model set the stage for a host of followers such as K-Mart, Sears and Roebuck, Target, Costco, and more.

In contrast to global manufacturers described in Option #4, big box stores do not produce any of the products sold in their retail stores. Rather, the stores comb the globe for cheap producers of the products the operators think will sell in their locale and then import these products. In this case, big box stores are nonasset corporations, meaning they do not own the factories that produce the items sold in their stores.

While the model is simple, getting things from foreign countries into the United States is not simple. The U.S. Department of Homeland Security and the Bureau of Customs and Border Protection must approve and screen every item that enters the country. Any business engaged in importing products to be sold in their stores must have in-house expertise about how these agencies operate in order to adhere to the policies and procedures associated with importation.

For example, items that are imported into the United States may be subject to an import tax, known as a **tariff**. We are all familiar with the concept of taxes, as each time we purchase an item in a big box store, we must pay a consumption tax that varies from state to state. The U.S. International Trade Commission in Washington, DC, presents a very detailed listing each year of the specific tariffs that must be paid when importing items into the U.S. for commercial  purposes, called the Official Harmonized Tariffs Schedule. Thousands of tariffs are included in the listing.

There are two standard types of import duties, or tariffs. The first is a specific U.S. dollar amount that must be paid for each item imported. Each wristwatch your business imports, for example, would incur a 51¢

import duty. The second type of tariff is an ad valorem tax, which is a percentage of the worth of the product being imported (i.e., total cost of the product plus freight and insurance). While each watch you import costs you 51¢, a case or strap for a watch is charged an ad valorem tax of 6.25 percent and a watch battery 5.3 percent. For the year 2018, the U.S. International Trade Commission reports that the average tariff was 2 percent on merchandise imports.

Becoming a specialist in import tariffs is a great career path that enables you to work with a host of businesses engaged in imports and exports. You will also become familiar with the vast array of products produced, exported, and imported each year, which is growing in size and scope quickly.

Option #6: Overseas Operations

As we move forward with further options for you to go global with your business, you will see that the level of complexity expands. We began with going global options that enabled you to continue to live and work in the United States (e.g., global licensing and foreign direct investing) and then progressively added layers of complexity (e.g., global M&As, global manufacturing, and big box stores).

Option #6 is even more interesting by virtue of it being the most global in terms of physical operations. Take the example of a U.S.-based factory that has successfully demonstrated its ability to produce products to sell to a loyal customer base in return for positive profits distributed to the stakeholders. Based on such success, your business may decide to consider moving its entire factory to another country.

This is a big decision that would engage your business in new and exciting ways. You would need, for example, to decide what country to consider and whether you want to rent space for your manufacturing facility or lease land on which to build a new facility. You would need to hire someone familiar with human resource policies and practices in the host country. You would need to establish relationships with new bankers. You would need to consult your existing employees to see who might be interested in moving to another country. The list goes on.

But if you do decide to move your entire operations overseas, your engagement with global commerce expands. For example, you would need to rethink where to secure the inputs for production in the overseas factory. Indeed, you could choose to keep using your loyal U.S.-based suppliers, some of whom may have supplied your business with inputs for many years. In this case, you would need to explore the costs associated with shipping and importing those supplies into the new country. Another possibility, not exclusive of the first, is to find some suppliers who are closer to where you now operate. This could include suppliers in the host country as well as suppliers in neighboring countries.

Once you have successfully started up your new overseas factory and are producing products, your next task is to think about customers. Hopefully, you will find a way to continue to sell to your loyal customers who have come to rely upon your products. In this case, you will incur the added costs of exporting your products from the new plant back to the United States. In addition, you might explore the option of developing a new customer base in the host foreign country.

While the example above pertains to a manufacturing facility, the notion of overseas operations applies equally to the service industries. All of the major U.S. banks, for example, have successfully established overseas operations to provide financial services to a global customer base (e.g., Citigroup, JP Morgan Chase, Bank of America, and Wells Fargo).

Just as U.S. businesses have engaged in overseas operations, so have foreign businesses set up operations in the United States. An example is the grocery business. With the post–Great Recession expansion boosting business coffers, foreign businesses began to look into capitalizing on the U.S. boom. One such leader was Lidl, a German discount chain. In 2017, Lidl opened nine stores in Virginia, North Carolina, and South Carolina, and anticipated opening another 90 new stores, an announcement that caught the attention of U.S. retailers Kroger and Walmart.

Lidl (est. 1973) is following the lead of their German rival, Aldi (est. 1961), which opened 1,600 stores in 35 states over the past four decades. The customer base of both firms is low- and middle-class shoppers seeking deep discounts on groceries. One of the key differences between

the German Lidl and Aldi grocery store model and their U.S. competitors is that the German stores sell about one-tenth the number of items. The German stores are also privately held, offering more decision-making flexibility for managers than their large publicly traded competitors.[4]

Option #7: Global Franchising

While the list of options for going global could continue, we'll end with global franchising, which is similar to the global licensing option we started with, only with a twist. Franchising is a form of business-to-business licensing; however, I believe it warrants examination as a separate option because it is a unique and popular form of licensing and an option you might consider if you want to start and run your own business.

Every year, Franchise Direct, a national franchise association in the United States, releases its *Top 100 Global Franchises* list. The rankings reflect a host of variables, such as the number of franchise units, revenues, stability and growth, number of years in operation, and expansion. The February 2019 release listed the following ten businesses at the top of the list:

No. 1	McDonald's
No. 2	Burger King
No. 3	Pizza Hut
No. 4	Marriott International
No. 5	KFC
No. 6	Dunkin'
No. 7	7 Eleven
No. 8	SUBWAY
No. 9.	Domino's
No. 10	Baskin Robins

---

[4]The Economist. June 15, 2017. "German Deep Discounters Go Big in America," p. 122.

What do you notice immediately about the top global franchisors in 2019? Nine out of the ten are incorporated in the United States, suggesting the United States has the jump on this concept of global franchising. In case you are wondering, the loner is 7 Eleven, incorporated in Japan.

How does a global franchise work? It starts with a business owner, called the *franchisor*, who might own a chain of restaurants in the United States but wants to expand globally. One possibility is for the owner to go to a foreign country and set up overseas operations, as we discussed in Option #6. This would be going global; however, it would be difficult for the owner to be in more than one place at a time. So, the person may decide to sell a franchise license to a *franchisee* in a foreign country.

The franchisee pays a license fee to the franchisor plus franchising royalties as determined and agreed upon between the two parties. In return, the franchisee in the foreign country receives help from the franchisor to set up and successfully run operations. Such assistance could include: training on how to lay out and run the store, marketing by the franchisor, public relations assistance, a trademark, the brand name use, management skills, special recipes, and access to suppliers used by the franchisor.

If you are ready to start your own business but do not have a specific business idea, you might consider running your own franchise business and benefit from all that the franchisor can offer to get you on your way. In return for all the assistance provided by the franchisor, the franchisee agrees to abide by the provisions of the franchise agreement (e.g., how to make McDonald's French fries a very specific way) and the franchisee provides the labor and capital to run the business. The franchisee operates the franchise business as a sole proprietorship.

As the largest global franchisor, McDonald's is planning further expansion. As aptly portrayed in a 2017-released film *The Founder*, the McDonald's start-up story by founder Ray Kroc is legend. Kroc's dream is manifest today in more than 14,200 McDonald's

restaurants across the United States and another 22,000 in 110 other foreign countries. Currently, 83 percent of McDonald's restaurants are franchised, but CEO Steve Easterbrook wants to increase that number to 95 percent. He does not think the firm should own and operate many restaurants, a cultural shift for a firm that prided itself on owning its own restaurants since the start.

In 2016, Easterbrook sold 1,750 company-owned stores in China for $2.1 billion to a consortium of China's CITIC Group Corporation, a state-owned investment firm, and the private equity firm Carlyle Group. McDonald's retains 20 percent ownership for the next 20 years. Whomever the consortium refranchises with to run the restaurants will pay royalty payments of 5 to 7 percent of sales. With fast-food stores moving from densely populated major cities into China's countryside, the firm believes it is advantageous to franchise with local partners who know local consumer tastes.

This new refranchising global growth model is one to watch in our search for options to go global.

Wrap Up

The above options for going global are by no means exhaustive as there are many other options or a combination of options to consider. This list, however, gives you a sense of what it means to go global with your business interests.

CHAPTER 6

Entrepreneurship

In this chapter, we explore another *functional area of business*, namely entrepreneurship and small business development. This takes us on a journey of discovering new ideas and possible ways to bring those ideas to fruition in the form of a new business entity, a new service or product, and/or a new business model that makes money.

Generating Ideas

All businesses begin with an idea. When coupled with a drive to get the idea out to the public, these ideas can lead to success stories. How do businesspeople come up with ideas? Is everyone successful? What are some of the key factors to consider to be a successful entrepreneur? What are possible risks associated with setting up your own business?

When asked, all entrepreneurs have stories to share as to the inception of the idea that resulted in their successful businesses. For some, the key was being a keen observer of people, society, and human behavior.

They figured out what would capture peoples' interest at a point in time. They were curious to learn what products people have been tired of and thus would be less likely to continue purchasing. They discovered what other entrepreneurs did to turn ideas into thriving enterprises. They learned, through acute observation and study, what ideas failed and why.

> All entrepreneurs have stories to share as to the inception of the idea that resulted in their successful businesses. For some, the key was being a keen observer of people, society, and human behavior.

Other entrepreneurs report that their ideas were born out of necessity that spawned creativity. Ideas are often grounded in rigorous research and development (R&D) and formal education. Yet other ideas emanate from a person's jobs, interactions with friends, cultural traditions, a slow hunch, or even a passion (or hobby) that consumes many waking hours. Below we examine overarching themes expressed by businesspeople regarding the sources of their ideas and how scientific inventions found their way into successful new products, services, business models, problem-solving, and marketing techniques.

Imitation

For some entrepreneurs, new ideas build on existing products (or services) that are copied or tweaked in a way that takes an idea to the next level.

Travel is a great way to seek ideas for businesses. Travellers observe people and their changing tastes, which sometimes wend their way into new product ideas. Business people who travel keep their eyes open for laudable ideas worth imitating, which may save time from trying to constantly create new concepts.

Global business management professor Oded Shenkar proposes that "Imitation is faster, cheaper, easier to implement, less risky, and more profitable than innovation—and you can imitate legally and profitably."[1] The business adage "innovate or die" has gone by the wayside among some risk-averse investors and producers who would rather put their energy into a tried-and-true product, practice, or business model than to start from scratch.

Through mechanisms described in the previous chapter, globalization fuels the imitation model of entrepreneurship as we increasingly live in an interconnected business environment in which we are constantly exposed to each other's ideas and lifestyles.

Invention–Innovation Partnerships

Invention entails the discovery of new science, which usually requires an enormous amount of time and money. For some entrepreneurs, envisioning

---

[1] O. Shenkar. 2010. *Copycats: How Smart Companies Use Imitation to Gain a Strategic Edge* (Boston, MA: Harvard Business Press).

brand-new discoveries that can be turned into lucrative products and/or services is what excites them most.

Take, for example, Yin Qi, chief executive of Beijing-based **Megvii** (standing for mega vision), one of the world's largest facial recognition firms. At Megvii's headquarters, a video camera installed in the lobby reads the faces of employees waiting for an elevator and identifies each person by name. Megvii has become a $2-billion business since 2011 by selling its proprietary facial recognition hardware and software (Face++) to 300,000 clients.[2]

Once faces are recognized using Face++, the images may be connected to other data, making the technology potentially valuable to a wide variety of businesses across numerous industries. Along with speech recognition equipment installed on handheld mobile devices, facial recognition is a burgeoning and potentially very profitable industry today. This is why in May 2018, HSBC, the largest bank in Hong Kong, introduced online facial recognition login to HSBCnet for retail customers in 24 countries.[3]

China's Megvii facial recognition business exemplifies the value of private for-profit business entrepreneurs partnering with public sector (government) entities to advance a new idea. The Rosetta Stone that enables Megvii's software to recognize the image of an individual person's face is its access to the Chinese government's image database of 700 million citizens collected for national identification cards. In this partnership, the government provides the facial database and Megvii provides the surveillance cameras and identification software that track human behavior, making the Chinese government a valued customer of Megvii.

[2]The Economist. September 9, 2017. "Visual Computing: The Facial-industrial Complex," p. 83.

[3]C. Hodgson. May 9, 2018. "HSBC Rolls Out Facial Recognition for Mobile," *Financial Times*. https://www.ft.com/content/acc823c0-52a6-11e8-b3ee-41e0209208ec, (accessed May 9, 2018).

Another valued facial recognition customer is China's e-commerce giant Alibaba's Ant Financial, which offers a "Smile to Pay" service that works like this: A customer wishing to purchase an item looks at a computer screen that takes her picture; the service then identifies the customer and electronically bills her bank account.

Facial recognition hardware and software are an integral part of autonomous humanoid robots, like the one I teach with in my business classroom.[4] Once installed in a person's home as, say, a family robot, the manufacturer collects images of the faces of family members and others who enter the home. Such information is valuable when paired with myriad other data collected in homes and workplaces to predict and interpret human behavior.

The application—or commodification—of facial recognition technologies by Megvii and its contemporaries is seemingly endless and hence worth the time and expense to foray into this new business terrain.

The global pharmaceutical industry demonstrates how innovators, inventors, and even imitators can work together. In Mumbai, India, the drug manufacturer, **Piramal Healthcare Solutions**, has for years copied patented drugs made by firms such as U.S.-based **Abbott Laboratories**. To overcome the imitation problem, Abbott purchased the pharmaceutical division of Piramal in 2010 for $3.7 billion (nine times its annual sales).[5] Today, Abbot's Piramal not only manufactures generic drugs for Abbot but also conducts R&D in India on new pharmaceuticals at a much lower cost than performing such research in the U.S.

Imitation, innovation, and invention have partnered in a way that benefits both parties. "The India story is an attractive growth story, but globally and in emerging markets, there is a new way of selling drugs

[4]P. Flynn. 2017. "Autonomous Humanoid Robots as a Pedagogical Platform in the Business Classroom," *Journal of Social Science Studies* 4, no. 1, pp. 178–88.
[5]The Economist. January 7, 2012. "The Drug Industry: Battling Borderless Bugs," p. 55.

(patented products), which we would not have been able to do on our own," notes Ajay Piramal, chair of Piramal, to which Abbott's chair and CEO, Miles White adds, "This strategic action will advance Abbott into the leading market position in India. The deal will complement our market-leading proprietary pharmaceutical offerings and pipeline in developed markets."[6]

The Internet of Everything

Innovation can also be interpreted as taking inventions and applying them in novel ways. A great example is the concept of the **Internet of Things** (IoT), whereby tiny computer sensors are embedded into evermore products that we bring into our homes and workplaces. Such devices are capable of automatically and wirelessly connecting to the Internet, which enables manufacturers to track exactly where a product is, how it is used, and by whom. Internet-connected objects include clothing, shoes, personal home-care products, medical devices, cleaning supplies, and even food.

The 130-year-old German giant Bosch prefers to be called "the Internet of Things company," having fully embraced the transition to becoming a firm that makes  money not only by producing high-quality German products but also by becoming a custodian of computational data. Peter Schnaebele, Bosch's senior vice president of the Smart Homes Unit, said, "Orwell's [novel] *1984* is kindergarten compared to the IoT-world. When it comes, and people re-evaluate privacy, Bosch will be prepared."[7]

Workplaces are also being built with tiny computerized sensors that detect a person's presence through heat and/or motion readings. Several big banks report installing sensors to track the work patterns of employees

---

[6]The Times of India. May 22, 2010. "Abbott Buys Piramal's Pharma Arm for $3.7bn." https://timesofindia.indiatimes.com/business/india-business/Abbott-buys-Piramals-pharma-arm-for-3-7bn/articleshow/5960176.cms, (accessed May 22, 2010). This is the 2nd-largest deal ever in the Indian pharma industry, just behind Daiichi Sankyo's takeover of Ranbaxy in 2008.

[7]The Economist. November 11, 2017. "The Internet of Things: Bish Bash Bosch," p. 59.

by monitoring the use of computational devices and tracking time at the desk.[8] Next we will shop at grocery stores where sensors installed on every item will communicate directly with each shopper's mobile devices. More on that when we explore the cutting edge of marketing using new developments in predictive data science.

The Internet of Things concept expanded in 2018 to become the "Internet of Everything" concept as even our brains could one day connect to the Net through brain-computer interfaces (BCI). Brain surgeons are experimenting with sophisticated ways to harness the firing of some 85 billion neurons in the brain. Doctors can already pick up high-resolution brain signals through EEGs (electro encephalograms) that read brain activities through a person's skin, bone, and membrane.

But what if medical doctors could secure even clearer signals by implanting electrodes under the scalp, directly on the surface of the brain's cortex to detect signals from brain neurons? Such BCI connections are in development by the U.S. Department of Defense and firms such as Neuralink, Kernal, Brain Gate, Neurables, Facebook, and NeuroLutions.

If successful, selected brain neurons could be harnessed to control external devices. Gamers anticipate the ability to use EEG caps to play virtual-reality escape games. Facebook has 60 engineers who envision using BCIs to simply "think" a text, rather than type a text. With the advent of artificial intelligence, human capabilities will have to be upgraded through intelligence augmentation (IA) if humans are not to be left in the dust.

In other words, neurons are a new resource to be mined by entrepreneurs in partnership with neurosurgeons. Brain-computer interfaces will meld the human mind with the computerized machine, taking the concept of the Internet of Things to new heights. The applications are limitless, notes leading BCI neurosurgeon and founder of NeuroLutions,

---

[8]The Financial Times. September 2-3, 2017. "Sensors and Sensibility: How Citi Tracks Desk Use," p. 27.

Dr. Eric Leuthardt: "This has the potential to alter the evolutionary direction of the human race."[9]

Survival Rates

Are you excited about the possibility of being an entrepreneur to get such ideas into the hands of interested customers? Do you have some new ideas that you want to explore? If so, you may be ready to launch your own enterprise by establishing one of the three types of business structures explored earlier: sole proprietorships, partnerships, and corporations.

But first, let's consider the risks associated with small business development. The U.S. Department of Labor's Bureau of Labor Statistics (BLS) provides valuable data on the survival rates of businesses registered with the U.S. Internal Revenue Service in the United States. The BLS reports that among all registered businesses, 66 percent are still in business 2 years after being registered by the IRS. To some, the fact that two-thirds of businesses make it to the 2-year mark is encouraging. To others, this statistic reveals that one-third of new businesses close within 2 years.

There could be myriad reasons why a business would close its doors. On the upside, a person may simply realize that business is not for them and voluntarily closes its doors. Another person may decide to shift gears and start another business in an entirely different industry. Someone else may decide to apply to graduate school and close down the business during this period of study.

On the downside, a person may not have been as successful in business as anticipated. Perhaps some uncontrollable factors negatively impinged on the business, as was the case for many owners during the Wall Street financial crash that began in 2007. Others may have experienced mild success in business but had not yet reached the breakeven point and hence were forced to shutter their businesses.

But if your business is among the 66 percent of businesses that are still in operation at the two-year mark, what does the future hold? According the BLS, after 5 years, half of all businesses remain open. Thus, it seems

---

[9]A. Piore. January/February, 2018. "The Surgeon Who Wants to Connect You to the Internet with a Brain Implant," *MIT Technology Review* 121, no. 1, pp. 45–59.

that 5 years is the midpoint when, on average, half of businesses are successful and half go out of business.

The BLS further calculates that, on average, 31 percent of businesses in the United States are still operating after 7 years. What are some of the factors contributing to business survival? The most important is financial success, followed by managerial success. Other factors, in no particular order, relate to planning, operations, human resources, location, timing, and global capitalism. And, of course, we cannot forget just plain old luck. We can only guess how many really hardworking people with great ideas and ample resources come up against hard luck in the world of business through no fault of their own.

Thus, consider carefully the industry in which you would like to establish your new business. If your focus is in any way related to digital products or services, beware. A study by *The Economist* reported that a full 42 percent of the rise in U.S. stock valuations between 2014 and 2017 were attributed to large Silicon Valley firms that have eviscerated many smaller businesses.[10]

Taking on the digital platforms requires deep pockets, as firms such as IBM and Walmart have learned from what they term being "Amazoned." In response, large incumbents are adding digital dimensions to their product and service lines. For example, General Motors and Target are focusing on e-commerce, big data, and artificial intelligence to capitalize on the fact that nondigital large firms own some 80 percent of all the commercial world's data, beyond the reach of the digital giants Amazon and Google. Other established firms are engaging in high-stakes mergers and acquisitions to include Walt Disney's acquisition of 21st Century Fox and CVS Health's merger with Aetna, both very high-dollar strategies to beat the incoming competition. Such incumbents are well-placed to be aggressive when competing with digital giants given that "their cash flow is four times that of tech firms' and 18 times what venture capitalists invest each year."[11]

My inclusion of data on survival and failure rates is not to discourage you from going into business but rather to give you a heads-up and reminder

---

[10]The Economist. January 6, 2018. "The Year of the Incumbent," p. 49.

[11]*Ibid.*

that business is not for risk-averse individuals, something to consider when setting up your own business.

U.S. Small Business Administration

Before concluding this module on entrepreneurship and small business development, there is one additional important resource to know. In 1953, the U.S. government established an office to serve small business owners called the U.S. Small

Business Administration (SBA). With its headquarters in Washington, DC, plus regional and district offices across the country, the SBA is a valuable resource for those wishing to start and run a small business.

How do you know if you qualify as a small business? The definition is established by the SBA and factors in three components. First, the business cannot dominate a field or industry. Hence, Amazon would not be considered small businesses. Second, the SBA sets a cut-off in the number of employees that a business hires to be considered a "small" business. Third, there are caps on the annual receipts (in USD) that a business can bring in to be considered "small."

The caps on number of employees and total annual receipts vary from industry to industry. Manufacturing and mining firms, for example, qualify as small businesses if they have no more than 500 employees. In contrast, the cut-off for wholesalers is only 100 employees. With regard to sales revenues, the cut-off is $750,000 for agricultural business, $7 million for retailers, and $14 million for special trade contractors (Figure 6.1).

The first step when establishing your own businesses is to check the website www.SBA.gov to determine whether your firm qualifies as a small business. It is potentially valuable if your business qualifies as a "small" business in the eyes of the Small Business Administration (SBA). If so, you are eligible to attend SBA trainings in the various functional areas of business to help you deepen your knowledge in areas where you could use assistance. Business executives and retirees often offer their services for free to help small business owners get started. Training is offered in a wide range of areas from bookkeeping and accounting to marketing and management.[12]

Another advantage of being considered a "small" business is that you may qualify for special SBA-guaranteed business loans through commercial banks and credit unions to help start and/or grow your business. Such loans are advantageous in that they require smaller down payments and allow longer repayment periods relative to commercial banks.

"A size standard, which is usually stated in number of employees or average annual receipts, represents the largest size that a business (including its subsidiaries and affiliates) may be to remain classified as a small business for SBA and federal contracting programs. The definition of 'small' varies by industry."

Source: Small Business Administration. www.sba.gov

Figure 6.1 Defining "small" business

Small Business Profile

Every year the U.S. Small Business Administration Office of Advocacy creates profiles of small businesses at the national and state levels, describing small business activities.

According to the SBA:

The Office of Advocacy's Small Business Profiles are an annual analysis of each state's small business activities. Each profile gathers the latest information from key federal data-gathering agencies to provide a snapshot of small business health and economic activity. This year's profiles report on state economic growth and employment; small business employment, industry composition,

---

[12]See the Small Business Administration's Learning Center for online and face-to-face courses: https://www.sba.gov/tools/sba-learning-center/search/training.

and turnover; plus business owner demographics and county-level employment change.[13]

For the year 2018, the SBA identified a total of 30.2 million small businesses in the United States, representing 99.9 percent of all businesses with payroll. Almost 59 million employees worked for small businesses, representing 47.5 percent of the private sector workforce. Some 62 percent of all net new jobs created between 1993 and 2016 were in small businesses.

Other interesting characteristics of the small business sector include the following:

- 36.3% are women-owned;
- 29.3% are minority-owned
  (12% Hispanic, 10% African American, and 7% Asian);
- 14.4% are immigrant-owned;
- 19.3% are family-owned; and
- 50% are home-based.

The U.S. Small Business Administration statistics and reports underscore how rich and varied small businesses are in the United States, suggesting that you will be able to find your place therein.

Ease of Doing Business

How easy is it to conduct business in the United States as compared to other nations? An indication is found in the World Bank's annual report titled "Doing Business," which compares the ease of conducting business in 190 of the 195 nations on Earth.[14]

For the year 2019, the World Bank reports that the country in which it was the easiest to start and run a business was New Zealand, the same as in 2016, 2017, and 2018. The United States, in contrast, ranked number

---

[13]For more details, see https://www.sba.gov/advocacy/2017-small-business-profiles-states-and-territories.

[14]The World Bank. January, 2019. *Doing Business 2019* (Washington, DC: International Bank for Reconstruction and Development).

8 in 2019 (#6 in 2018). Factors that are tracked include the ease with which a person can start a business, obtain construction permits, get electricity, and register property. The rankings pay attention to year-on-year changes in the regulatory environment in each country and the effort made to attract and support in-country business development, factors that will impact how successfully your new business may be wherever you plant roots.

Wrap Up

With this backdrop on entrepreneurship and small business development, next we will explore the all-important money side of starting and running a business, including financial management, equity financing, and debt financing.

CHAPTER 7

Financial Management

Once you have envisioned a business idea, established yourself as an entrepreneur or secured a job with a business in your industry of interest, and assumed the attendant risks of running a business, what's next? It is time to talk about money in order for you to realize your goal of earning a profit.

There are many financial questions that present themselves at this point in the business process. If you are starting out on your own, you might consider how many months (or years) you can support yourself until your business is self-sustaining. If you need money, where do you go? What is this place called Wall Street? How does it work? How do you get people to invest in you and your ideas? If you are going to borrow money, when do you have to repay it? How will you handle growth of your business from a financial perspective? What do people who decide to study finance end up doing on the job?

What Is a Business?

An organization
comprised of people
who produce goods and services
to sell
to earn a profit
distributed to stakeholders

This and the next two chapters will help you decide if the field of finance is for you and, if so, what area(s) of expertise to pursue. In the end, you might decide that you do not necessarily want to become a financial expert but rather pursue work in another functional area of business.

Even so, it helps to know a little about money and banking because we live on a planet where global capitalism impacts every person, business, and corner, no matter how distant or small.

So, it pays off to be informed about money and finance. Every business needs money to succeed, be they large transnational corporations, mid-sized established busi-

> It helps to know a little about money and banking because we live on a planet where global capitalism impacts every person, business, and corner, no matter how distant or small.

nesses, or new small enterprises. We need money to start a business, stay in business, and grow a business. Money is the oil that greases the wheels of business.

We define business as an organization, comprised of people, who produce goods and services, to be sold, in order to earn a profit, distributed to stakeholders. The finance functional area gets to the heart of earning a profit, which is where we begin.

Careers in Finance

One of the benefits of becoming a financial expert is the array of jobs available across all industries. In the private for-profit world of business, finance is a requirement to succeed as a chief executive officer (CEO) today. This was not necessarily the case in the past when an individual who was well-versed in a particular product or service could establish and run a business without having a lot of knowledge about finance, which could be handled by associates skilled in finance. This is no longer the case. Every CEO today starts the day combing through financial data pertaining to one's business and industry. Hence, studying finance is a must for those seeking to be a chief executive one day.

Chief financial officers (CFOs) are also responsible for the financial functioning of business. The CFO works nonstop on matters related to money, banking, and financing of the business. That said, given the data intensity of business today, I learned being a CFO that we are privy to an enormous amount of information that goes beyond just finance, to include strategy, operations, human resources, and logistics. Thus, while overseeing the finance department, the CFO plays a controlling role in broader aspects of a business. This is why the median pay for a CFO employed by an S&P 500 company was $3.4 million in 2016, with Charter Communications' CFO paid $29.2 million![1]

Banks also hire people with expertise in finance, including bank presidents, bank officers, and consumer credit officers. The best way to begin a career as a financial executive in a bank is to start as a bank teller, who is responsible for the daily handling of cash and frontline customer needs. In the investing industry, financial experts fill positions such as financial analysts, financial planners, and investment account executives. These experts are responsible for handling other people's money as well as the investment house's own proprietary investments.

During the 2010s, we saw growth in a particular type of investment specialist called a registered investment adviser (distinct from a financial adviser, who brokers the sale of stocks and/or bonds). RIA professionals must be registered with the Securities and Exchange Commission or a state's securities agency to provide investment advice to individual clients. According to the Investment Adviser Association, annual "assets under management at registered investment adviser firms grew 5.8% to $70.7 trillion, and the number of firms increased by 2.7% to 12,172" as of April 1, 2017.[2] The enormous size of the portfolios managed by RIAs is notable: $70.7 trillion versus $20 trillion in total U.S. annual gross domestic product in 2018.

Accountants are trained financial experts who perform necessary bookkeeping, tax filings, and financial reporting for businesses of all types. Professional accountants have passed a state examination to hold a Certified Public Accounting (CPA) license. Comptrollers are also trained accountants as are forensic accountants, who specialize in financial fraud detection and more.

Financial Management Process

If you are considering becoming a financial manager for a business, what would your job entail? In a nutshell, the financial management process proceeds in four steps, as follows.

---

[1]Equilar. August 25, 2017. "Highest-Paid CFOs Exceed $20 Million in Total Compensation." https://www.equilar.com/blogs/299-highest-paid-cfos-2016.html, (accessed September 20, 2017).
[2]Investment News. August 1, 2017. "Assets at RIAs Growing at 5.8%," p. 3.

Step #1: Establish Clear Financial Goals with Your Client

Step #1 requires spending time with your clients, usually members of the board of directors, the chief executive officer, and other senior executives, to clarify exactly what they want to see happen in the short-term vis-à-vis the firm's finances. Is this a year where new facilities will be built? Is a merger and acquisition envisioned? Is a division shut down in the works? Is there a specific return on investment desired by the directors?

The financial goals must be realistic, which is your job to ensure. Big thinking is great; however, our job as financial managers is to be sure that the goals are achievable from a money perspective, which demands tough conversations and careful deliberations. Securing consensus on the short-term financial goals among the executives may take several meetings over a long period of time. The extra effort to ensure everyone is operating on the same page is well worth the energy; otherwise, there could be a lack of clarity across the business as to where the firm is headed.

Step #2: Prepare a Draft Budget

Once the short-term financial goals are agreed upon, Step #2 of the financial process is for you to prepare a draft budget. This requires seeking detailed estimates of the projected income over an agreed-upon period (e.g., one calendar year) alongside projected expenditures during the same period. As the financial manager, you may have to train staff in the various divisions of the business on how to come up with budget estimates, a job that will pay off in subsequent accounting cycles.

Step #3: Conduct a Budget Analysis

This step entails analyzing the data collected in Step #2 and determining whether the business will have sufficient funds to realize its goals over the specific period in question. It is important to stress that your budget analysis will only be as good as the data that were provided by division managers on projected income and expenditures. This is where it pays off to work closely with division managers and teach them how to devise solid estimates.

The answer to the question posed in Step #3 (will the business have sufficient funds to realize its goals?) is binary. If yes, you are concluding that to the best of your knowledge and data, the business will be able to meet its financial goals for the period in question. In this case, your job is to present the findings to the executives and carefully monitor the books week in and week out to be sure the actual income and expenditures do not veer far from the projected income and expenditures.

Step #4: Consider Possible Financing Mechanisms

If the answer to the question posed in Step #3 is no, then you are concluding that the business will not, in all likelihood, be able to meet its financial goals, which leads us to Step #4: consider possible financing mechanisms. Before you share the bad news with the executives, I recommend that you devise some ideas as to how the business might achieve its financial goals. After possible financing mechanisms are discussed and a financial plan is approved, you and your financial management division will secure the necessary financing and monitor the progress benchmarked to the financial goals established in Step #1.

Wrap Up

The next two chapters will explore in depth financial mechanisms to help finance business activities grouped into two options: equity financing and debt financing.

CHAPTER 8

Equity Finance

All business owners need money—known as financing—to establish a firm, to operate daily, and to grow in whatever ways the owner deems best.

Two of the most common forms of financing are **equity** and **debt**. The value of equity financing is that the money people invest in your business does not come with a promise that it be repaid. Debt financing, in contrast, requires repayment with some type of compensating interest, as negotiated. This chapter provides examples of equity financing, followed by examples of debt financing in the next chapter.

What Is a Business?

An organization
comprised of people
who produce goods and services
to sell
to earn a profit
distributed to stakeholders

Equity finance is a form of financing in which you convince other people to invest money directly into your business. This money could be used for myriad purposes, ranging from building a new office, developing a new product, paying off debt, purchasing equipment, hiring workers, buying inventory, to paying off accounts receivable.

Securing equity finance requires aggressive fundraising on your part as the owner or the responsible party representing someone else's business.

Anyone with money to invest is a possible source of equity financing, such as other business owners interested in your firm, individual investors, or the owners of the business itself.

Equity investors own a part of your business and expect to be financially rewarded if the business is a financial success. Let's look at five types of equity finance common to business: owner's equity, shareholder's equity, retained earnings, venture capital, and assets.

> Anyone with money to invest is a possible source of equity financing, such as other business owners interested in your firm, individual investors, or the owners of the business itself.

Type 1: Owner's Equity

Owner's equity is a straightforward, quick, and simple way to raise money for a business. This is money that an owner, say the person who started the business, puts into the business to get it up and running or to expand. It is common for people starting their own business to have saved up enough money to invest in the start-up of a new firm for an initial period of time. If the firm is a partnership, each partner could invest owner's equity in the business, as needed.

It is important to note that any money that partners put into the business in the form of owner's equity is not a loan to be repaid to that partner. The owners are investing their own money with the assumption that the business will be successful and reap rewards in the form of significant profits and job security, for example, in the future.

Type 2: Shareholder's Equity

Shareholder's equity takes form through the sale of shares of stock in a business. Each stock is sold to an investor who pays a specific price per share. The money the investor pays for the stock serves as shareholder equity that the business may use in myriad ways.

Closed versus Open

Not all businesses can legally sell stock. Corporations and limited liability partnerships have the advantage of being able to issue and sell stock to raise funds. If you decide to set up your business as a corporation, you must decide whether your firm will be closed or open. A **closed** business is one in which the ownership of the firm is privately held by the owners and a small number of private investors. The public is not allowed to purchase shares in a closed corporation.

In contrast, if you want anyone to be able to invest in your business and acquire shareholder equity, then you will opt to establish your business as an **open** corporation, also known as a publicly traded corporation. In this case, you must choose an exchange where the buying and selling of stocks takes place through brokers and traders. Famous exchanges include the New York Stock Exchange (owned by Intercontinental Exchange), NASDAQ, Japan Exchange Group, Shanghai Stock Exchange, Hong Kong Stock Exchange, Shenzhen Stock Exchange, London Stock Exchange, Euronext in Europe, TMX Group in Canada, and Deutsche Börse in Germany.

If you decide to become an open corporation, who can you solicit to invest in your business through the purchase of your stock? In today's world of finance, the majority of stockholders are institutional investors, that is, other businesses that invest money in a specific firm via a stock exchange. Examples of institutional investors are bank trusts, mutual funds, hedge funds, endowments, insurers, and pension funds. A minority of stocks held today are purchased by individuals who invest their personal money in stocks, known as retail investors. Almost 80 percent of the stock of corporations listed in the S&P 500 index today is owned by institutional investors, with the remaining owned by individuals.

Common versus Preferred

Why would a person spend their hard-earned money on a stock that comes with no promise to repay the money invested? Usually, investors buy stocks that they believe will realize an increase in the price per share over and above what they paid initially. Thus, when it comes time to cash in, the person will realize a capital gain.

The very first time a business allows the public to buy its stock is called an initial public offering (IPO), also known as "going public." Prior to an IPO, the business must decide what type of stock it will sell. Most often, businesses will differentiate between the sale of common shares and the sale of preferred shares.

The difference between common and preferred shares is revealed at the firm's annual stockholder's meeting. If your business sells stock to the public, it is required by U.S. law to hold a stockholder's meeting at least once a year and to notify stockholders beforehand. The meeting is a way to learn about new ideas, products, services, or strategies envisioned by the board of directors and senior executives. It is also a place where shareholders can pose questions of the owners and operators of the business. Anyone who holds common or preferred shares is invited to attend the annual shareholders meeting and will receive a written invitation along with salient items to be discussed.

At the annual meeting, stockholders will be presented with specific items that require a vote, such as deciding who will serve on the board of directors and other matters pertaining to governance, operations, and business policy. Who is allowed to vote on such matters? Only common shareholders. Thus, while preferred shareholders may attend the annual shareholders meeting, they are nonvoting shareholders.

What then makes preferred shares *preferred*? One advantage of holding preferred shares is the preferential claim to business assets and earnings in the event, for example, of a bankruptcy. In this instance, a business will sell off its assets for payout to various stakeholders. First to be paid are bond holders, followed by other creditors, then preferred shareholders, and lastly common shareholders. Shareholders who invest in preferred stocks also do so because such shares may provide a steady source of income through dividend payments. Preferred stocks usually receive higher dividend payments than common shareholders.

One of the topics of great concern each year among shareholders is the amount of money the business will distribute to shareholders in the event the business is profitable. Such distributions are known as **dividends**. Both common and preferred shareholders are eligible for dividend payments, but no one is guaranteed to be paid dividends. Only the board of directors can determine whether a firm will distribute dividends to shareholders and, if so, the amount of the dividend. At the annual meeting, a representative of the board of directors may tell shareholders of its intention to pay dividends at the end of the coming year if profit targets are met (or exceeded), but the board has the right to change its mind in the interest of the business.

In sum, common shareholders are invited to the annual shareholders meeting, may vote on issues presented, and are eligible for dividends. In contrast, preferred shareholders are invited to the annual shareholder's meeting and are eligible for dividends but hold nonvoting shares.

Type 3: Retained Earnings

In addition to owner's equity and shareholder's equity, a business also may raise equity capital through retained earnings. At the end of each year (e.g., calendar year, fiscal year), your accountants will present to you and your partners a summary of all financial activities that transpired. The accountants will calculate the total revenues that came into the business throughout the year from all sources. They will then subtract the total costs accrued throughout the year by all expense categories. The balance is your business' annual net profit.

Before you start thinking about all the things you will do with those profits, your accountant will remind you of the pledge made to pay dividends to shareholders in the event you are an open corporation. Once dividends have been paid, the remaining sum of money is called *retained earnings*.

Retained earnings are a form of equity financing that you may invest in your business. It is a simple and direct way to raise money quickly to cover financial needs. And it is cost-free as any money left over after dividends have been paid are yours to keep or reinvest in your business.

Of note are historical trends in the payout of dividends by corporations in the United States. From 1900 to the 1970s, an average of two-thirds of profits were paid out in the form of dividends, thus encouraging investors to put their money into shares of stock with the assumption that significant dividend payments would be received at year's end. During the 1980s and 1990s, only one-third of profits were paid out in dividends, on average. During and immediately following the Great Recession, many corporations stopped paying dividends altogether.

Post-2012, some of the major transnational corporations slowly resumed paying dividends, albeit at historically low levels. The result is more cash for use as retained earnings and fewer investors seeking dividend payments on their shareholder equity investments. During the 2010s, this cash windfall was used by many businesses to buy back their own stocks. As such, many corporations demonstrated a preference for moving away from being open corporations (with stock available for purchase by the public) to being closed corporations (with stock privately held).

Type 4: Venture Capital

Venture capital (VC) is money raised from wealthy investors, be they institutions or individuals, who hope their investments will yield significant short-term profits. This type of equity financing is unlike shareholder's equity in that you are not selling a tangible stock that serves as an investor's claim on the business. Nor is the money coming from a founder or owner who has a vested long-term interest in the firm. Venture capitalists may know very little about you or your business except a notion that whatever goods or services you are producing may pay off handsomely one day soon. But they have money and want to invest quickly in technology novelties.

As a result, new small technology firms are able to raise large quantities of money from venture capitalists seeking the next big invention, rather than raising money through stock offerings. The result is that VC-funded firms can stay private for long periods of time and avoid initial public (stock) offerings, lengthening the time before venture capitalists can get their money out. The longer the wait to sell stocks, the higher the risk for the venture capitalist equity investors.

What might a venture capitalist want in return for giving a business its money? Some might demand ownership in the funded firm, such as becoming a limited partner. Some might want privately held preferred stock (with an option to convert to common stock) and a promise of being first in the queue to sell those shares when the business makes its initial public offering or is bought out in a merger and acquisition. Remember that venture capitalists are not necessarily interested in the long-term welfare of your business, but rather short-term gains.

Type 5: Assets

The fifth and final example of equity finance in this module is a last resort. If your firm really needs cash and has had no success fundraising through owner's equity, shareholder's equity, retained earnings, or venture capital, you are left with the last resort, which is to sell the assets owned by your business.

I left this type of equity financing for last because, as a rule, you do not want to rely on selling assets to keep your business moving forward. In fact, it may be very difficult to operate fully if you start selling assets such as trucks, buildings, and inventory. However, if you are in dire straits and want one more push to raise equity financing to propel your business forward, by all means, go ahead and sell some of your assets and use the money in this time of need. After all, that is why we have assets.

Notable Trends

There are three notable trends when it comes to equity finance mechanisms.

First, in the United States, fewer firms are deciding to sell shares to the general public. In 1996, there were 7,322 businesses listing their stock on public exchanges. By 2017, that number was down to 3,671. More businesses are avoiding initial public offerings (IPOs). Why? Because there are new sources of equity from wealthy individuals, private equity firms, and venture capitalists who are willing to provide small firms with financial capital.

New and highly valued firms are staying private longer, making it difficult to buy into a business you deem to be a potential winner unless you are privy to a private placement (or sale) of stock to a small number of chosen investors. Some of the most cutting-edge research in novel technologies, such as autonomous humanoid robots, augmented reality, artificial intelligence, brain-computer interfaces, genome editing, voice-control interfaces, virtual reality, facial recognition, and chat bots, are off-limits to most investors until there is an IPO.

The infamous founder of Uber, Travis Kalanick, touted, "I say we are going to IPO as late as humanly possible. It'll be one day before my employees and significant others come to my office with pitchforks and torches."[1] Kalanick indicated that he did not need shareholder equity for Uber, which was then valued at $41 billion, almost four times the $11-billion value of the entire taxi industry in the United States. After Kalanick was ousted as CEO in 2017, Uber's Board of Directors held an IPO at the New York Stock Exchange on May 10, 2019, yielding the business $8.1 billion in equity.

A second notable trend in equity financing is the sale of **nonvoting shares** by a corporation. Nonvoting shares allow the founders to retain control of business operations, governance, and decision making while at the same time raising equity. On April 2, 2014, Alphabet issued a zero-voting-rights type of stock (e.g., "C" class), leaving founders Larry Page and Sergey Brin owning the majority of voting shares in their business, a move that caught the attention of other digital platforms. Facebook followed suit and issued nonvoting shares in June of 2017. The decision benefits Mark Zuckerberg, founder and 70 percent shareholder of Facebook, who can use his nonvoting shares as a form of money to pay for mergers and acquisitions or as donations to tax-exempt entities while retaining the majority of voting authority in his firm.

The advent of "C" shares is not without controversy. In July 2017, Standard & Poor's (S&P) and FTSE Russell said they would no longer include firms with multiple share class structures (including non-voting shares) in their benchmark indices. S&P's stated reason for the new policy is that "Companies with multiple share class structures tend to have corporate governance structures that treat different shareholder classes unequally with respect to voting rights and other governance issues."[2] For the time being, S&P will allow existing multiple share index constituents, such as Facebook, Alphabet, and Under Armour, to remain in the S&P indices.

The March 2, 2017, initial public offering of Snap Inc. (est. 2011) was the first *all* nonvoting-shares IPO in U.S. history, which blocked Snap

---

[1] R. Milne. October 12, 2016. "Norway's Oil Fund Warns over Lack of IPOs," *The Financial Times*, p. 14.

[2] CNBC. August 1, 2017. "Snap is falling again as Wall Street worries about the company's corporate structure." https://www.cnbc.com/2017/08/01/snapchat-excluded-from-sp-500-what-does-it-mean.html, (accessed August 1, 2017).

from being added to the S&P 500 Index. Its founders, Evan Spiegel and Bobby Murphy, set up the nonvoting share "C" class structure to insure their control of the business through a closed governance model.

The Securities and Exchange Commission overseeing equity finance in the United States noted that the practice of shifting to nonvoting shares "raises the prospect that control over our public companies, and ultimately of Main Street's retirement savings, will be forever held by a small, elite group of corporate insiders."[3] One idea being discussed to limit outsized founder voting power is to establish a rule whereby businesses must retire their dual-share structure after a limited number of years rather than upon the death of the founder or longtime controlling shareholder.[4]

Wrap Up

Never a dull moment in high finance!

---

[3]The Wall Street Journal. February 16, 2018. "Regulator Targets Firms with Dual-Class Shares," p. B1.

[4]*Ibid.*

CHAPTER 9

Debt Finance

When looking for money to finance your business, you have many options. In our society, it is easy to think immediately about borrowing money to realize your ambitions. While debt can be a solid solution to your financial concerns, it is not the best place to start looking for money. Hence, we began our discussion about financing with equity capital in the previous chapter. You may want to consider fully the options available to you and your business in the form of equity capital, including owner's equity, shareholder's equity, venture capital, and retained earnings, before venturing into debt financing.

If you still need money, then it might be time to consider borrowing.

There are times when debt is the best option, but only if you realize the risks involved and can make good on your promise to repay the money owed.

Below is a discussion of short-term debt, which must be repaid within one year, and long-term debt, repayable in more than one year, depending on the agreed-upon terms. By the end of this chapter, you will have a good sense of the pros and cons of going into debt to finance your business start-up, ongoing operations, and/or growth strategy.

> There are times when debt is the best option, but only if you realize the risks involved and can make good on your promise to repay the money owed.

Short-Term Debt Financing

Short-term debt financing is borrowed money that must be repaid within a year, depending upon the agreement made between the borrower and the lender.

Type 1: Secured Debt

The first type of short-term debt is called **secured debt**. In the event that someone is considering giving you a loan for your business, you may be asked to present the lender with some kind of collateral that will make the lender whole if unable to repay the borrowed money.

Think about what you own that you would be willing to put on the table—and possibly lose—in the event you default on the loan. For example, do you own a car that you could put up as collateral? Do you own a home? Do you own any inventory or a building you could use as collateral? Determining what form of collateral will meet the needs of the potential lender is a matter of negotiation. Put your best foot forward when making a case for your credit worthiness. But do not be offended if the lender decides it is vital for you to post collateral in return for a short-term loan.

Type 2: Unsecured Debt

Every lender is different. Not all require collateral, a decision based on a host of factors, such as a borrower's credit score, track record repaying previous loans, and income history. If you do not look like a financial risk, you may not have to post collateral to secure a short-term loan. The lender may be willing to issue you an **unsecured short-term loan** with no required collateral.

One example of unsecured short-term debt financing is **trade credit**. Trade credit is an excellent way to delay payment to a supplier for 30 to 60 days. Trade credit occurs when a business regularly orders from a supplier merchandise to be sold in, for example, a retail store. Rather than paying the supplier the moment the merchandise is delivered, trade credit provides the business with a short window of time to come up with the money to pay its supplier. In the United States, more than three-quarters of businesses have established trade credit agreements with their suppliers.

Let's examine how deliveries work without trade credit. Suppose you own a retail store that receives regular deliveries of goods from your supplier that will be displayed and sold in your store. On the day merchandise is delivered to the store, you will examine the merchandise, sign for the delivery, and pay the driver an agreed-upon amount of money for the merchandise. That completes the transaction.

If you and the supplier have a trade credit agreement, the process changes. On the day the merchandise is delivered, you examine the contents, sign for the delivery, and receive an invoice from the supplier listing all items delivered and the amount of money owed. On the bottom of the invoice, you will see a statement that will look something like the following: 2/10, net 60. What do these numbers mean? The 2 means that you will be able to deduct 2 percent of the total amount due if you pay for the delivery within 10 days. Otherwise, you must pay the full amount for the delivered merchandise within 60 days.

In other words, the supplier is offering you a 2 percent savings if you pay for today's delivery before the 60-day trade credit payment date. Trade credit is a wonderful short-term debt financing mechanism because it gives you time to actually sell the merchandise and earn the money to repay the supplier. In other words, trade credit is free money! No interest is due on the money owed.

Some trade credit short-term debt financing agreements are for 30 days, the longest being 60 days, depending upon what you and your supplier agree upon. If you are able to take advantage of the discount offered by the supplier and pay before the end of the 30-to-60-day window, by all means do so. Every little bit of savings helps.

A second example of unsecured short-term debt is a **promissory note**. What if you need more than 60 days to repay a supplier for the merchandise you will be selling in your store? You could negotiate a promissory note, which is a promise to repay the lender within an agreed-upon period of time. Usually, promissory notes require repayment in no longer than 180 days (i.e., 6 months). This gives you considerably more time to sell the merchandise in your store and earn the money to repay the supplier relative to a trade credit arrangement.

In return for having more time to repay the supplier—up to 180 days—a promissory note requires that you pay the money owed with interest accrued over the entire repayment period. This makes sense given that the supplier needs some type of monetary compensation for loaning you the money until payment is received.

Take your time negotiating the details of a promissory note repayment plan and put the terms of the agreement in writing to be reviewed and signed by both the lender and the borrower. There is no such thing as a verbal promissory note. There is no such thing as a handshake deal with a promissory note. A promissory note is a legal and tradable instrument, binding you to pay the money owed within the agreed-upon repayment period plus an agreed-upon rate of interest. The lender in this case does not require the borrower to post collateral, hence promissory notes are another example of unsecured debt.

A third type of short-term debt is an **unsecured bank loan**. One of the things that you will want to know when shopping for a banker for your business is whether the bank provides business loans and the specific terms therein. If the bank issues short-term business loans, how much time does a business owner have to repay the loan? How much interest would a borrower have to pay the bank for the loan? How often will the business have to make payments on a short-term unsecured loan? All these questions need be to be explored and negotiated by the borrower and lender.

There are times when a banker may require you to provide some type of assurance that you will repay the loan. Some banks will only issue secured loans. In the absence of collateral, a bank might require that you have a certain amount of money in a business savings or checking account with the same bank. As with all short-term loans, the bank will expect repayment within 12 months, per the agreed-upon terms of the loan.

A fourth type of short-term unsecured debt is **commercial paper**. Commercial paper is borrowed money that must be repaid in no longer than 12 months. It is also a promissory note, meaning a promise to be repaid, without posting collateral.

Commercial paper is a debt-financing tool commonly used by large businesses, especially corporations, to raise money quickly. A business may need, for example, money to fill a cash flow gap in the months leading up to the Christmas season and could sell commercial paper in order to have sufficient funds to increase its inventory. Commercial paper also could be sold to raise funds to pay large accounts receivable, short-term liabilities, and even payroll, depending on the needs of the firm at a certain point in time. Commercial paper is usually not used for fixed assets (e.g., a new office or plant).

In order to raise short-term commercial paper funds, a business posts a notice of its intention to sell its "paper" to the general public and/or other businesses. Buyers of commercial paper include wealthy individuals, money market funds, financial institutions, and other large corporations seeking short-term investments. Usually commercial paper will be repaid in less than or equal to 270 days (i.e., 9 months). The average length of commercial paper debt instrument in the United States is 30 days. No collateral is required to be posted.

Commercial paper became very popular in the United States beginning in the 1990s. The value of outstanding commercial paper was $500 billion in 1991 and rose to $1.58 trillion by 2005, peaking at $1.78 trillion in 2007, just before the Wall Street financial crisis. By mid-2018, the value of outstanding commercial paper was $1.1 trillion.

The difference between commercial paper and standard promissory notes is the manner in which lenders are compensated. Most firms sell commercial paper in lots of $100,000, which would be the "face value" of the note payable in, say, 270 days. However, on the day the commercial paper is sold, the business will receive from the lender less than $100,000, which is the "par value." The difference between the face value and the par value is the money the lender earns by lending the borrower money through the sale of commercial paper. This form of short-term debt financing is thus considered a non-interest-bearing note because the lender does not technically earn interest on the loan, but rather is compensated the difference between the agreed-upon par value (the dollar amount loaned) and the face value (the dollar amount repaid).

Long-Term Debt Financing

In addition to short-term debt instruments (i.e., secured and unsecured), businesses might seek long-term debt financing for projects that are more ambitious and may take considerable time to reap the anticipated financial rewards. Long-term debt financing is borrowed money that must be repaid with interest in more than one year, depending upon what is negotiated between the lender and the borrower.

Below are two types of long-term debt financing instruments: bank loans and corporate bonds.

Long-Term Bank Loans

Long-term bank loans are similar to short-term bank loans in that they provide needed financial capital to businesses that promise to repay the loan with interest. Each bank sets the terms of its loans, including the amount of money it will lend a borrower (i.e., the principal amount), the length of time a borrower has to repay the loan (i.e., the repayment period), and the amount of interest a borrower must pay the lender as compensation.

Commercial banks and cooperative banks usually set interest rates in sync with monetary policies set by the Federal Reserve, the central bank of the United States. Interest rates also will reflect the perceived financial risk of each potential borrower. If you seek a long-term bank loan, the bank will conduct a credit check on your firm's credit worthiness before determining the terms of the loan. Rarely will a bank require collateral to issue a long-term business loan.

Corporate Bonds

A second source of long-term debt financing for a business is through the sale of a corporate bond. This is a common mechanism used by big firms to raise large amounts of money, at times billions of dollars, from other businesses, institutional investors, and individual investors.

Suppose you have saved some money and would like to invest it in a business that you see is growing and/or holds tremendous potential. For whatever reason, you do not want to buy stock in that business, which would involve an equity transaction. Instead, you decide to loan the business some of your money by buying one of its corporate bonds. As a result, you expect to be repaid in an agreed-upon amount of time and to receive interest payments on the money you have loaned through the bond sale.

Corporate bonds are long-term investment vehicles that can be held for 10, 20, and sometimes 30 years. This is a long time to have your money tied up if you are a corporate bond holder. The longer the time period for the bond, the more interest you can expect to earn on the money you lend to the business. As a corporate bond holder, you are now a creditor, meaning you have a claim on the business's assets in the event that the firm goes bankrupt.

In Chapter 5, we discussed the M&A negotiations surrounding Verizon Communication's purchase of all of Vodaphone's stock in Verizon Wireless. In September 2013, a deal was struck whereby Verizon Communication agreed to pay $130 billion to Vodaphone, resulting in full ownership of Verizon Wireless. So where did the $130 billion come from? Turns out Verizon Communications successfully issued a corporate bond for $49 billion to help pay for the M&A. This was the largest corporate bond issue ever in history, on the heels of Apple's record corporate bond of $17 billion earlier in 2013. Per the terms of the bond issue, those who purchased bonds from Verizon Communication will be repaid in 16 years.

Corporate bonds are a steady source of debt financing for corporations. Globally, corporate bonds reached a new high of $9 trillion in 2019. As businesses take on more corporate debt, they also are extending the bond maturities (i.e., the repayment period) in order to lock into historically low interest rates. It is no longer uncommon to hear of corporate bond issues to be repaid in 100 years, called century bonds.

Wrap Up

These are very interesting times for debt financing given 10 years of near-record low interest rates and a resulting rush to finance investments through debt. For some firms, their financial arms are growing faster than their production arms. A case in point is Apple, one of the world's largest digital platforms.

Digital platforms have amassed enormous financial wealth since the Wall Street financial crisis, enough to threaten the nation's largest financial firms and perhaps ultimately impact national economic stability. Apple, for example, holds $262 billion in assets, $108 billion in corporate bond debt, and has traded $1.6 trillion in financial securities between 2011 and 2017. Apple's financial reach is extraordinary.

The firm's strategy is to keep profits from foreign sales and subsidiaries abroad to avoid paying U.S. corporate income taxes. "Some 94% of Apple Capital's assets are offshore and cannot be tapped for ordinary purposes," reports *The Economist*.[1] To pay dividends and stock buy-backs, Apple's domestic business borrows money. By 2017, Apple's "domestic net debts [rose] to $92 billion, or five times domestic gross operating profits. To finance its debt, each year Apple must issue $30 billion in

---

[1] The Economist. October 28, 2017. "Apple Capital LLC," p. 65.

bonds, similar to the average of Wall Street's largest firms."[2] Balancing its massive production of iPhones with its enormous financial activities is the name of the game for Apple Capital.

Has Silicon Valley's debt binge gone too far? Minutes from the Federal Reserve's 2016-2018 Federal Open Market Committee meetings "expressed concern that the protracted period of very low interest rates might be encouraging excessive borrowing [in] the nonfinancial corporate sector. As the long period of low interest rates continued, cheap borrowing costs prompted more borrowing. Much of that went to fund shareholder-friendly activities such as dividend increases and share buybacks. It also funded big mergers and acquisitions."[3]

Another trend to watch is the changing role of **private equity firms**. As the name suggests, such firms provide equity capital to businesses in exchange for the potential to make great sums in the event of an initial public offering (IPO) or other payouts as negotiated. In recent years, however, private equity firms have aggressively become lenders to businesses in need of money for mergers and acquisitions. With so much money-chasing buyout deals in the 2010s, some of the traditional lenders (e.g., banks) stopped lending for buyouts, and private equity firms stepped in.

The shift is notable: traditional retail bank loan funds managed about $100 billion in 2018 compared with private credit funds (including private equity firms), which manage $650 billion in assets—three times more than in 2007.[4] The upshot is that some private equity investors are providing both equity financing and debt financing simultaneously, sometimes for the same businesses—a risky strategy.

In the end, it is valuable to understand the various types of equity and debt financing mechanisms available to new and established businesses in order to weigh the risks and benefits of seeking outside money to support your business goals.

---

[2]*Ibid.*

[3]The Wall Street Journal. October 17, 2016. "Investors Unfazed by Borrowing Increase," p. B3.

[4]The Wall Street Journal. February 16, 2018. "Rise of Private Assets is Built on Mountain of Debt," p. B1.

CHAPTER 10

Big Data

In the past few years, business schools around the world began offering degrees in a new *functional area of business* known variously as big data, data science, data analytics, and business data. Because of advances in data collection on all aspects of our lives over the past 20 years, businesses are able to influence customer behavior at a level that would make the Ad Men of the twentieth century envious. Previous advertisers relied on broadcasting their messages in the hopes of capturing the ATTENTION of potential customers. Today, big data enables advertisers to micro-target those customers most likely to buy their products and services. Big data is a game changer in today's business environment!

This chapter describes this new phenomenon sweeping the planet. We will explore how big data grew out of advances in computer hardware and software. We will consider how computer algorithms micro-target and "nudge" customers using predictive analysis. We will study businesses that have created far-reaching networked digital supply chains that connect businesses directly with individual customers through handheld mobile devices. We will examine the beacons used at retail stores to directly access customer mobile devices for merchandising and pricing. We will consider how the human experience data collection business translates into profits.

Big data is an exciting new field. If you are considering a career in marketing, sales, advertising, and/or public relations, understanding this new functional area of business is the place to start your exploration.

The Cloud

To understand big data, we need to return to the mid-1990s with the advent of what is now called cloud computing. The pioneer in cloud computing was Bill Gates, founder of Microsoft in Silicon Valley, California.

After making a fortune selling Microsoft hardware and software, Bill Gates turned his attention to the trove of data his firm had amassed. He considered how his customers could access data that Microsoft stored on their network of servers.

Given that few people use computer science lingo, Gates came up with the term "the cloud" for customers to envision a cloud of data in the sky that could be accessed from any location, regardless of where the servers and customers where physically located. He announced that users could now store and access their data that sat in "the cloud" wirelessly

 through Web browsers (e.g., Firefox Mozilla, Microsoft Internet Explorer, and Google Chrome).

The term "cloud computing" stuck. As Microsoft's customer databases grew, so did the size of the cloud of data collected on all of the online activities Microsoft customers performed.

Data storage and computing, however, is not cheap. Microsoft pays for huge networks of servers capable of storing customer data. Initially, customers were able to access some of their personal data from the MS cloud for free. The next step was to figure out how to use customer data to make money, specifically how Microsoft could *monetize* the data collected on customers' online activities.

Microsoft began to post suggestions to its customers, pointing to other products that a person might be interested in buying based on past data collected online. From here, computer scientists started writing predictive algorithms that followed some type of logic whereby if a consumer purchased products A, B, and C, then s/he might be interested in purchasing products D, E, and F.

Microsoft's brilliant cloud computing concept impelled other large firms to start collecting and creating clouds of data on their customers' online and in-store activities. Google founders, Sergey Brin and Larry Page, saw the vast potential and purchased the YouTube video-streaming site in 2006 for $1.65 billion. Mark Zuckerberg, founder of Facebook, realized he was sitting on a gold mine of data collected on now 2.4 billion people across the planet who post data on Facebook accounts. Zuckerberg believed his "cloud" of user data would be quite valuable to the right marketers. Internet Service Providers (ISPs), to whom users pay monthly fees to access the Net, realized that they too had an enormous store of data, unique to each customer, which could be monetized. Large retail stores also saw the value of the "cloud" of data they collected on every purchase made by every customer who shopped at their stores, dating back to the introduction of personal computing.

Large retailers also sought to expand personal customer data in lucrative ways. But how? They asked themselves how they could utilize the enormous amount of information gathered on all the activities a person performed on the Net or inside a store. Who would want the data? And, more importantly, who would pay big data firms for such data?

Enter the Marketers

This is where the marketers entered the picture. Historically, marketers have done their best to broadcast product advertisements in locations where potential customers might see the ads in order to capture people's attention (such as radio and TV broadcasts, print publications, billboards, etc.). This is an expensive proposition but was perceived as necessary to reach a broad pool of potential buyers.

But what if marketers could go to a big data business and purchase a list of names of people who exhibit certain traits and behaviors associated with an existing customer base? Such a list would be quite valuable for marketers who, it turned out, would pay dearly for such data to be used to micro-target specific customers.

Forget broadcasting; micro-targeting became the new frontier for advertisers. By the 2010s, almost every child, young adult, and adult in the United States carried a handheld supercomputer in the form of a mobile device. After purchasing selected data from a big data broker, marketers could send ads directly to the palm of a potential customer's hand. It's that easy to reach customers today and in

turn collect personal data. Did you ever wonder why when you pay for an item in a retail store, the cashier nonchalantly asks you for your e-mail and phone number, as if this information were required to complete the transaction? Harnessing micro-data directly from customers gets easier day by day and screen by screen.

The Value of Customer Data

Is this a win-win business strategy? Big data firms are paid handsomely for their cloud-based data and predictive behavioral analysis. Retailers that collect enormous amounts of data on customers have persuaded the courts to treat customer data as a financial asset during bankruptcy proceedings. Marketers have been very successful with micro-targeting campaigns using data purchased from big data firms.

Who is missing from this data supply chain? The people whose everyday lives are being surveilled. The value of customer data leaped to the forefront of national discourse on April 10–11, 2018, when Facebook CEO Mark Zuckerberg testified before the U.S. Senate and U.S. House of Representatives in Washington, DC, following the revelation of a major leak of data on 87 million Facebook users. A London-based political consultancy firm, Cambridge Analytica, owned by Robert Mercer, harvested private information on Facebook users without their consent to build voter profiles during the 2016 presidential election.

This was made possible because Cambridge Analytica hosted a third-party app on Facebook's platform that allowed for the tracking of Facebook users' and friends' account data. Rather than addressing the issue when it was first brought to light in 2015, Facebook threatened to sue the journalists who revealed the data heist. As the eighth largest business in the world (valued at $471 billion as of March 2019), Facebook resists any restrictions on developers' access to data on Facebook's digital platform.

The topic of unauthorized digital platform data dissemination will increasingly be the focus of business interests in the near term. In order for the big data model to be lucrative, the supply chain of incoming data from human experiences must continue to be free.

Hence, the mountains of consumer data now collected are the most treasured commodity of the twenty-first century and requires significant storage facilities.[1] As of 2018, leaders in the big cloud industry by revenues were: (1) Amazon Web Service, (2) Microsoft Azure, and (3) Alphabet's Google Cloud Platform, all incorporated in the United States. Their major competitors are Alibaba Cloud (in China), IBM Cloud Computing, and Oracle's Big Data Platform.[2]

Big Cloud Industry

#1: Amazon Web Service

#2: Microsoft Azure

#3: Alphabet's Google Cloud Platform

#4: Alibaba Cloud

#5: IBM Cloud Computing

#6: Oracle Big Data Platform

Both the United States and Europe are actively seeking ways to protect personal data from being bought and sold. As of 2018, users in the United States have no right to opt out of data collection or dissemination by digital platforms or third-parties.[3] By contrast, Europe scrutinizes digital platforms to protect data since the passage of privacy laws in 1995. On April 27, 2016, the European Union adopted the General Data Protection Regulation (GDPR) introducing "a new set of *digital rights* for EU

---

[1]In 2010, Facebook built a data center on a 124-acre site in the desert of Prineville, Oregon. The first building is as long as an aircraft carrier; the second is slightly bigger. Nearby, Apple built an iCloud data center on a 160-acre site, close to facilities owned by Google, Amazon, Rackspace, and Bend-Broadband for cloud computing. See Andrew Blum's book titled *Tubes: A Journey to the Center of the Internet* (New York, NY: HarperCollins Publishers, 2012) on the building of data centers to accommodate the growth in data worldwide and attendant enormous demand for electricity 24/7 to keep the racks of servers from overheating.

[2]See Gartner. 2018. *Gartner's 2018 Annual Report on Cloud Computing.* https://www .gartner.com/en/products/special-reports.

[3]For an overview of how ad-financed digitally networked platforms gather, disseminate, and monetize user data, see Zeynep Tufekci's book, *Twitter and Tear Gas: The Power and Fragility of Networked Protest* (New Haven, CT: Yale University Press, 2017).

citizens in an age of an increase of the economic value of personal data in the digital economy" (Regulation EU 2016/679). The new law went into effect on May 25, 2018.

Wrap Up

What is new for big data? Shoshana Zuboff makes a compelling argument in her book, *The Age of Surveillance Capitalism*, that a new business model is in the making.[4] During the first two decades of the twenty-first century, the emergent business model was data collection and full-blown micro-targeting, described above. Now that our whole lives are searchable, what's next? During the coming decades, Zuboff argues that the existing surveillance system will use the enormous amounts of data collected on the human experience to "nudge" people toward certain behaviors.

Google is leading this effort, having created a massive virtual supply chain of behavioral data from our everyday lives to include "searches, e-mails, texts, photos, songs, messages, videos, locations, communication patterns, attitudes, preferences, interests, faces, emotions, illnesses, social networks, and purchases" through the Internet's computer-mediated architecture (Zuboff 2019, 128–29). This represents the (free) acquisition of raw human material at a scale that can be rendered into new *prediction products* to be bought and sold in behavioral futures markets.

Can business perhaps rethink how to use digital data in such a way as to include the producer-consumers of the data itself in a more transparent and less adversarial fashion? Or is the business-consumer relationship in capitalist economies inevitably one of contention? Has promiscuous connectivity and data collection reached a point whereby users have slowly become acclimated to a system of constant surveillance, thus challenging democratic societies, as posited by Zuboff and media expert Siva Vaidhyanathan?[5] These are questions that business students and professors might want to examine together when considering the future of the big data *functional area of business.*

---

[4]S. Zuboff. 2019. *Age of Surveillance Capitalism: The Fight for a Human Future at the New Frontier of Power* (New York, NY: PublicAffairs).

[5]S. Vaidhyanathan. 2018. *Anti-Social Media: How Facebook Disconnects Us and Undermines Democracy* (Oxford, England: Oxford University Press).

CHAPTER 11

Marketing

With big data as an explosive new reality fueling sales, advertising, and merchandising, we now turn to an exploration of how marketers are responding.

Big data is the mechanism used by social marketers whose aim is to change human behavior, ideas, and attitudes within a targeted consumer group.

Successful marketers are astute observers of human behavior. They are skillful researchers, as demonstrated by the breakthroughs in big data collection and analysis. Marketers are also quick to adapt to new business environments.

They spend marketing budgets judiciously. They realize that the marketing *functional area of business* is critical to the overall success of the business. All eyes are on them.

Successful marketers are astute observers of human behavior. They are skillful researchers, as demonstrated by the breakthroughs in big data collection and analysis. Marketers are also quick to adapt to new business environments.

What Is a Business?

An organization
comprised of people
who produce goods and services
to sell
to earn a profit
distributed to stakeholders

Earlier we defined business as an organization, comprised of people who produce goods and services to sell for a profit to be distributed to stakeholders. The marketing *functional area of business* fits squarely into the **selling** part of our definition. If you are interested in sales and advertising, this is the functional area to pursue.

Being levelheaded, practical people, marketers see the external world in the binary: that which they cannot control and that which they can control. Examples of external environmental factors marketers realize they cannot control are the business cycle, the Great Recession, global capitalism, scientific inventions, and population demographics. To invest money in these elements is not smart in the minds of marketers.

In contrast, elements that marketers believe they have a shot at controlling are worth time, effort, and money. In 1960, University of Notre Dame Professor Jerome McCarthy came up with a catchy way to remember such controllable elements, dubbed the Four Ps: **product, place, price,** and **promotion.**[1]

McCarthy's topology treated the marketing functional area of business as a management science to help executives better understand consumer behavior. The Four Ps compressed the marketing process into a memorable construct and remains in our business lexicon 60 years later, a tribute to Professor McCarthy's deep knowledge of his field of study.

Below we examine the four marketing Ps with the aim of describing each element, exploring how the elements are changing in the twenty-first century and considering how the four Ps impact your buying habits.

Element #1: Product

To begin, the marketing department is charged with designing a strategy that encompasses marketing activities and programs that will support the business's intended end goals for a specified period of time. This strategy includes the first of the Four Ps: **Product.** Businesses must determine

---

[1]E.J. McCarthy. 1960. *Basic Marketing: A Managerial Approach* (Homewood, IL: R.D. Irwin).

what products they are going to sell. They must consider ways to differentiate their products from those sold by competitors. They will make every effort to attract customers in a highly competitive business environment.

Marketers consider, for example, who are the biggest buyers in society: women or men? What is your guess? If you guessed women, you could be on the brink of a successful career as a marketer. Women purchase between 70 and 80 percent of all goods and services in our economy.

Therefore, to be effective as a marketer, it is vital that you get into the minds and hearts of women; we buy the most stuff. Think about your moms who most likely bought your clothes, your food, your school supplies, your toothpaste, your sheets and towels, the furniture and appliances in your home, and much more. Women are famous for the amount of shopping done on Black Friday, the day after Thanksgiving. The marketers who came up with that blockbuster idea must be proud as this is one of the biggest commercial days in the United States.

The next question for marketers was how to get men to shop more. Marketers thus invented a day called Cyber Monday, the Monday after Thanksgiving, which aims to get men to shop online, a very clever strategy that has proven to be quite successful.

The Chinese have taken note of the success of Black Friday and Cyber Monday and, in 2016, created Singles Day to get single people to shop online. Singles Day falls on the 11th of November and is now the busiest shopping day in China. Alibaba e-commerce giant rang up sales of $18 billion on November 11, 2016, the most ever spent in one 24-hour period anywhere on earth! A year later, Alibaba's sales hit $25 billion on Singles Day, dwarfing Black Friday and Cyber Monday combined.[2]

This tremendous marketing success led the Chinese to expand their targeted customers beyond single people to include all online shoppers in China. The result is a new **11.11 Global Shopping Festival**, widely advertised by Alibaba. The 2017 launch in Shanghai featured celebrities such as Nicole Kidman and Pharrell Williams, offering special discounts

---

[2]A. Murray. November, 2017. "China's Singles Day Is a Shopping Extravaganza Heard around the World," *Time Inc.* https://www.scribd.com/article/364746736/China-S-Singles-Day-Is-A-Shopping-Extravaganza-Heard-Around-The-World, (accessed November 30, 2017).

on products from P&G, Estée Lauder, Starbucks, Bose, Nike, and Gap. On the 11th of November each year, shopping becomes a sport and a form of entertainment in China.[3]

Why would Alibaba go to such extremes to promote its 11.11 Global Shopping Festival? Because marketers know that the **product** element requires consideration of not only the tangible goods that customers may buy but also the intangible allure associated with specific products.

We have all been tempted to buy things not necessarily because of the actual product itself, but because of its appeal to our sensibilities, preferences, and dreams. That is why Alibaba paid handsomely to include Nicole Kidman in their first 11.11 Global Shopping Festival, knowing how many women admire this world-renowned actor's consumer taste and lifestyle. The allure of a movie star became the **product** Alibaba presented to its consumers in the hopes that they would be tempted to buy its tangible online products as a result.

Tim Wu, Columbia University law professor and marketing expert, has studied ways that attention brokers have effectively convinced us to view a **product** as more than meets the eye. Think about the notions of convenience and efficiency that have been marketed to consumers since the mid-twentieth century as valuable commodities. Buying a washer and dryer makes life easier. So does a microwave oven, automatic locks on car doors, and motion-detecting lights. Now that everybody has access to such products, Wu argues that twenty-first-century products are marketed to us as ways to express our *individuality*, a newly prized product in a world of mass-marketing.[4]

---

[3]The Economist. October 28, 2017. "E-Commerce: There Be Giants," p. 31.
[4]T. Wu. February 16, 2018. "The Tyranny of Convenience," *The New York Times*. https://www.nytimes.com/2018/02/16/opinion/sunday/tyranny-convenience.html, (accessed February 16, 2018).

As the marketer's notion of **product** became increasingly abstracted from the tangible product itself, the whole concept of *brand* exploded. It used to be that particular things that businesses manufactured and sold became brands, like Hamburger Helper or Kleenex. The Ad Men of the twentieth century helped businesses differentiate what they were selling from the glut of other products available for consumption. Nowadays, anything can be a brand when imbued with meaning such as a lifestyle brand (marketing a way of being) or a brand face (the way consumers see themselves while eating/wearing/using a product).

Even business entities themselves can become sellable brands when imbued with meaning. For example, after the 2016 and 2018 scandals at Wells Fargo were exposed, the bank's PR staff went into high gear. On May 6, 2018, Wells Fargo launched a massive ad campaign to aggressively rebrand the bank with a new tagline: *Established 1852. Re-established 2018 with a recommitment to you.* The actual products sold by the bank did not change. The aim was to regain the good will of its customers by trying to rebrand Well Fargo as a trusted bank so that people would feel differently about its banking products.[5]

Advertiser Dan Pallotta summarized branding in the *Harvard Business Review* as follows: "Brand is much more than a name or a logo. Brand is everything, and everything is brand."[6] In this way, our notion of the **product** marketing element takes new form and goes well beyond the notion of product differentiation.

Element #2: Place

Once you have established what you are selling, where and how are you going to distribute your products to people who might be willing to buy what you are selling? There are many ways to think about this second marketing P called **place**, and the strategies being tried are unlike anything we have seen before in the world of marketing.

---

[5]D. Roberts. May 7, 2018. "Wells Fargo knows customers are still frustrated. Here's what they're doing about it," *The Charlotte Observer*, p. C1.

[6]D. Pallotta. June 15, 2011. "A Logo Is Not a Brand," *Harvard Business Review*, p. 150.

One of the biggest changes in place-based marketing is the rapid growth of e-commerce, which impacts the retail, logistics, manufacturing, robotics, and marketing industries. The largest e-commerce firms are:

- **Amazon**, founded in 1996 in the United States by Jeff Bezos;
- **Tencent**, founded in 1998 in China by Ma Huateng;
- **JD.com**, founded in 1998 in China by Richard Liu; and
- **Alibaba**, founded in 1999 in China by Jack Ma.

E-commerce firms are a direct challenge to retail merchandising as people no longer exclusively associate shopping with stores and malls. Walmart, once queen of U.S. retailing, now pays China's Tencent and JD.com to provide the necessary infrastructure to support e-commerce (e.g., cargo planes, drones, voice assistants, cloud computing, retail stores, online stores, social media, and e-payment systems) as it switches channels from big box store sales to online sales.

Place-based marketing has several layers, from geographical to psychological, physical, virtual, and digital. Let's begin with *geographical* place. As the world becomes more interconnected through rapid advancements in global capitalism, businesses can find customers across the six major inhabited continents. Learning how to navigate this global arena is tricky and can be expensive.

In February 2012, the Michigan-based Kellogg Company (doing business as Kellogg's) purchased Pringles potato chips from Ohio-based Proctor & Gamble (P&G) for $2.7 billion in cash. Why? Kellogg's wanted an easy route to selling its cereals outside the United States. Kellogg's CEO John Bryant announced that "Selling cereal and selling snacks are two entirely different skills, it turns out. When it comes to overseas snacks, Kellogg's currently lacks chops. What the company is buying in Pringles isn't just a line of products that is already hugely international, but a group of P&G merchandisers with the snack mind set." The job of the staff at Pringles was to geographically place Kellogg's products in foreign countries.

For this reason, Kellogg's decided to retain the people who worked in P&G's Pringles advertising department after the 2012 buyout because they possessed the requisite skills to take Kellogg's global. Kellogg's is making headway, becoming a global brand and selling its products in some 160 countries.

A second layer of **place** is *psychological*. Marketers who study psychology find novel ways to influence how and what people will buy. If potential customers can be made to feel good or have a positive association with a particular product, they are more inclined to spend money on that product.

Such was the hope of Hollywood producers of the movie *Superman: Man of Steel* in 2013. The producers approached selected church pastors to promote the movie in exchange for cash and in-kind church donations. Pastors who agreed were given notes for their Sunday sermons, titled, "Jesus: The Original Superhero," to promote the movie.

Another layer of **place** is *physical*, the one most commonly associated with retail shopping. Where do you physically place your products in a store? Do you want your products to be on full view at the end of an aisle? Do you want specific lighting directly above your display? Do you want displays near the checkout counters? Are you willing to pay more to personally set up a display of your products in a store rather than leave it up to the store clerks?

Some businesses have taken the physical space concept to another level, whereby stores have been re-created as recreational spaces to encourage customers to play with new products for fun. Have you been to an Apple store lately or a Microsoft store where hard selling to customers takes a back seat to inviting customers to play with the new devices? These are examples of physical **place**-based marketing strategies.

Physical space advertising has reached new venues, including elementary and secondary public schools, where firms pay to cover school lockers with banner ads. Some schools have accepted advertisement dollars to place business ads on student report cards and permission slips.

Lady Gaga, the world-renowned musician, songwriter, performer, actor, producer, businesswoman, and media mogul, rocked the world with a new *virtual* marketing strategy upon creation of her Lady Gaga virtual community of fans. As described on her site, *www.littlemonsters.com*, Gaga announced to her millions of fans that she would be choosing a select group of 10,000 super fans each year who get one-stop-shopping for all things Gaga. The idea was a resounding success and propelled large transnational corporations, such as Nike and ExxonMobil, to approach Lady Gaga to help create virtual communities for their customers.

Last but not least of the **place** element is *digital* marketing, which is revolutionizing the world of business today, thanks to the advent of sensors (on products) and beacons (in stores) that connect marketers directly with their products and their customers 24-7 (via mobile devices).

Tiny computer chips and sensors are installed on manufactured items that enable a business to track a product from the factory, to the store, and to the end consumer. This is called the "Internet of Things" (IoT). The sensors on the packaging of soft drinks and soap power, for example, detect where a product is used and when to reorder the product. When a customer presses Amazon's Dash Button on a household item, the product is automatically reordered through Amazon Prime and mailed to the customer's home.

Athletic wear contains nearly invisible computer chips and sensors that collect medical vital signs data from the wearer's body (e.g., heart rate, pulse) to be stored in the firm's data cloud. The number of wirelessly connected products in existence (excluding phones and computers) is estimated to reach one trillion by 2035, up from 31 billion worldwide in 2020, and 15 billion in 2015.[7]

And wait until you see what's coming next in terms of the **place** marketing element: in-store retailers are installing a new type of computerized beacon inside stores that connect wirelessly with customers' mobile devices, a system called "geofencing." Retailers are able to track how long a person walks through a store, how much time is spent in each aisle, what products shoppers pick up, and whether or not a product

---

[7]The Economist. September 14, 2019. "Chips with Everything," p.13 and Statista. n.d. "Internet of Things (IoT) Connected Devices Installed Base Worldwide from 2015 to 2025 (in billions)." https://www.statista.com/statistics/471264/iot-number-of-connected-devices-worldwide, (accessed May 14, 2018).

is purchased.[8] The value of the data collected is the equivalent to a person's Web browsing history, as it reveals a great deal about personal preferences and shopping habits. Retailers also know where you are when you make purchases and can send you advertisements and coupons while you are literally standing in the aisle of a store, thinking about whether or not to make a purchase. If you decide not to purchase the item you were looking at, be prepared to receive a text message as you head home, enticing you to reconsider making that purchase.

Advancements in **place**-based marketing reflect a whole new approach to customers, merchandising, and sales. The focus is now on *personalized selling on an industrial scale*. Google calls its customized online advertisements "online behavior or interest-based advertising ... [that] helps support the free content, products, and services you get online."[9]

Consider, for instance, a flight attendant congratulating you on reaching 100,000 air miles while at the same time apologizing for the delay of your flight to Washington, DC, last week, offering you a complimentary gin and tonic—the same drink you had on last week's delayed flight—as a courtesy.

How did the flight attendant know this information about you and your travels? Airlines have a trove of traveler data on seat assignments, birthdays, credit cards, and the number of times a customer researched a flight on its website before booking.[10] Airlines are hoping to use these data to boost profits and mitigate against growing agitation associated with shrinking leg room, narrower seats, fees for luggage, no food service, and lengthy airport check-ins. Will having a friendly flight attendant—with a handheld device that contains your personal information—reach out to you personally make you feel valued? Or better yet, might it entice you to book another flight with this airline?

---

[8]J. Turow. 2017. *The Aisles Have Eyes* (New Haven, CT: Yale University Press).

[9]Terms of Service, www.google.com, (accessed May 15, 2018).

[10]C. Hodgson and P. Waldmeir. May 9, 2018. "Airlines seek to lift profit margins with big data," *The Financial Times*, p. 27.

The reality of these novel **place**-based marketing strategies—enhanced by big data—is that most consumers have no clue this is going on, thanks to what is called "black ops" advertising.[11] We are not supposed to know when we are the target of marketing. Is this lack of transparency necessary to be successful in commercial endeavors today? If marketers told customers their marketing strategies, would it still work to sell **product**?

Element #3: Price

Historically, merchandisers established the prices for products using the laws of supply and demand. General equilibrium theory teaches that the profit-maximizing **price** is where the aggregate demand curve for a product crosses the aggregate supply curve. Marketers knew not to price products so high that customers would be tempted to buy elsewhere, nor too low (i.e., below the firm's direct and indirect costs). Prices were then customized to accommodate the seasonality of a product, inventories, weather, location, and preferences of potential customers.

Once again, we see that big data and sophisticated computer-generated algorithms are changing business models. Today, marketers value customer data more than the **price** a person is willing to pay for a product. As the Silicon Valley adage reveals, if you are not paying for a product, you are the product, meaning the value of your personal data exceeds the cost of the service provided. Thus, price may be the amount of money a person is willing to pay for a product or service. But price also may represent intangibles that a person is willing to give up, such as time, effort, quality, and personal data.

So how do marketers price their products? With the rapid dissemination of in-store *beacons* that connect with the sensors installed on products that connect wirelessly with customers' mobile devices, merchandisers have their answer.

Computer scientists envision the day when marketers will no longer print prices on items. Instead, while a customer is standing in the grocery store aisle, marketers will send a digital message to a customer's mobile

---

[11]M. Einstein. 2016. *Black Ops Advertising: Native Ads, Content Marketing, and the Covert World of the Digital Sell* (New York, NY: OR Books).

device with a personalized price for a product based on the value of a person's shopping history data online and offline. Updating price tags will go from being a daily physical in-store ritual to a continuous computerized ritual conducted through artificial intelligence. Customers will not even know what other shoppers pay for the same product.

The Wall Street Journal reports that the big box retailer Target will spend $7 billion between 2017 and 2020 to revamp its stores with such wireless tracking devices.[12] Jones, Lang LaSalle (JLL), the world's second largest commercial property firm, recently cut a deal with Alexander Babbage to install geofencing technologies in their malls to "track shopping habits of consumers by analyzing the locational pings sent by their mobile devices and apps."[13] JLL's Pinpoint geofencing system is an aggressive effort to lure retailers into their shopping centers, knowing the mall has state-of-the-art wireless tracking hardware and software, viewed as a necessary part of marketing these days.

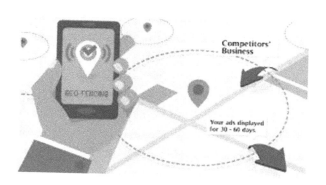

E-commerce, big data, beacons, computerized sensors, handheld mobile devices, and geofencing are revolutionizing the **price** element of marketing in ways Professor Jerome McCarthy could never have envisioned in the 1960s!

---

[12]C. Mims. April, 2017. "Three Difficult Lessons for Traditional Retailers," *The Wall Street Journal*, p. B1–B2.

[13]J.R. Parrish. December 12, 2017. "Real-Estate Firms Look to Technology to Figure out Shoppers," http://jrparrish.com/real-estate-firms-look-to-technology-to-figure-out-shoppers/, (accessed December 12, 2017).

Element #4: Promotion and Public Relations

The fourth marketing P is **promotion**. This is a vital piece of the marketing environment that focuses on advertising, publicity, propaganda, broadcasted ad campaigns, personal selling, sales promotions, protecting a business's image, and ultimately protecting the face of the business. At present, marketers commonly refer to the fourth element as public relations (PR) because the concept of product promotion has expanded significantly over the past half century. As a result, executives no longer hold the job title of Vice President for Promotion, but rather Vice President for Public Relations, Vice President for Public Affairs, Director of Communications, or Chief Customer Officer to reflect an integrated marketing strategy that blends the Four Ps together.

The **promotion** person is responsible for selling not only business products but also the business entity itself. S/he plays the vital role as the public face of a business. No wonder, PR executives are among the highest paid people in the for-profit business sector!

The Ad Men

Sophisticated advertising has its roots in the 1920s on Madison Avenue in New York City, where some of the big industries of the U.S. Industrial Revolution and post–World War II boom hired a nascent group of merchandisers called the Ad Men. Two pioneers were Edward Bernays and Albert Lasker, who fundamentally changed the orientation of merchandisers.

Edward Bernays was one of the most influential pioneers in the field of promotion. Born in Vienna, Austria, as the nephew of Sigmund Freud, Bernays came to the United States to begin a career in marketing while in his 20s. His first book, *Crystallizing Public Opinion* (1923), put him on the map. He challenged conventional ideas and persuaded marketers to mold opinions held by the growing working class.[14]

Bernays' ideas stuck and landed him on the cover of *LIFE* magazine as one of the 100 most influential Americans of the twentieth century. Edward Bernays loved his work so much that he continued as a PR consultant

---

[14]S. Ewen. 1996. *PR! A Social History of Spin* (New York, NY: Basic).

almost until the day he died, at the age of 104. Had Bernays been born a hundred years later, he would have recognized that big data is the new mechanism used by social marketers, whose aim is to change human behavior, ideas, and attitudes of a targeted consumer group through in-depth research and data collection.[15]

In addition to reading the works of Edward Bernays, anyone serious about becoming a public relations expert would benefit from studying the life's work of **Albert Lasker**. A contemporary of Bernays, Lasker changed commerce in the United States in the first half of the twentieth century with a host of innovative PR strategies delivered on behalf of his corporate customers as president of the famed Lord & Thomas advertising agency. Jeffrey Cruikshank and Arthur Schultz's book about Albert Lasker, *The Man Who Sold America: The Amazing (But True!) Story of Albert D. Lasker and the Creation of the Advertising Century*, aptly sums up the life of this famous PR man.[16]

The brilliance of Lasker can be found in the array of public relations strategies he designed to promote and sell products that U.S. businesses were manufacturing at an industrial scale never seen before, ready for purchase by the rapidly growing middle class. Lasker's Ad Men promoted the quest of business entities to wipe out the Ma-and-Pa sole proprietors and become nationwide retail chains, something we take for granted today. Lasker taught TV viewers to accept commercials in return for "free" entertainment, a precondition for digital platforms today. Lasker also formulated the field of political PR campaigns, unheard of prior to his successful campaign to reelect the governor of California in 1934, a PR technique ubiquitous in contemporary politics.

Lasker had his hand in a host of other pathbreaking campaigns that resulted in the creation of the fourth marketing P, **promotion**, which now includes public relations (PR). In his own words,

---

[15]See P. Kotler and G. Zaltman. July, 1971. "Social Marketing: An Approach to Planned Social Change," *Journal of Marketing* 35, pp. 3–12.

[16]J.L. Cruikshank and A.W. Schultz. 2010. *The Man Who Sold America: The Amazing (But True!) Story of Albert D. Lasker and the Creation of the Advertising Century* (Boston, MA: Harvard Business Review).

I was connected with the first advertising ever done on canned pork and beans, canned soup, canned spaghetti. When I with my associates conceived and financed the first advertising of tires; when I was of that group who first advertised automobiles; when with associates I defined advertising so that it became a force of social good to introduce to the people new and better ways of life, I could work inspired, because I was fulfilling myself.[17]

Lasker amassed a great fortune and lived to see a new age in advertising. In 1942 at the age of 62, this larger-than-life giant of PR closed the Lord & Thomas advertising agency and transferred his creative genius into promoting charitable causes he and his wife Mary admired. By the end of his life, Lasker—the original social marketer—was able to do something of "significance," in his own estimation, through advocacy and philanthropy.

Wrap Up

The famed Ad Man Albert Lasker "changed the way people understood the world—and thereby set the world on a better course."[18] How will you use the incredible tools offered through sales, advertising, merchandising, and public relations to make your mark on the world? How will you use your skills and knowledge to promote your version of the good? And lastly, how will you use your education to weigh the evidence, to discover the real from the unreal, and come to judgment on your own terms?

---

[17] *Ibid.*, pp. 346–47.
[18] *Ibid.*, p. 378.

CHAPTER 12

Management

This primer has focused on the fundamental building blocks of business, including legal structures, growth strategies, options for going global, entrepreneurship, small business development, equity and debt financing, big data, marketing, and public relations. We have covered a lot of material with the intention of grounding you in the key facets of starting and running a business.

What Is a Business?

An organization
comprised of people
who produce goods and services
to sell
to earn a profit
distributed to stakeholders

Now we come to our last *functional area of business*: **management**. I saved management for last because you already know something about this topic. We considered, for example, marketing skills that will enable you to manage your own careers in business. You understand the financial management steps necessary for those of you who go into finance. And you have your own experiences working with managers in paid jobs or volunteer service, during which you were able to observe bosses in action. Therefore, you will be able to approach this last functional area of business with some understanding of what management entails.

Management fits into our definition of business through the **people** who comprise a business. If you are good with people, you may want to consider a career in management.

Ultimately, management is about power, which explains why the topic is so intriguing and why there are many books written about managers.

Managerial power is key to business success in that it enables you to influence people and their decisions.

Power enables you to develop strategies you want to see implemented. Power enables you to hire the best people. Power enables you to motivate your staff. Power enables

> Managerial power is key to business success in that it enables you to influence people and their decisions.

you to be a role model for others. Power enables you to harness the necessary resources to achieve your goals. Managerial power will enable you to make the changes you want to see in the world.

The Economist magazine, a venerated business publication, launched a weekly column in 2018 devoted exclusively to management titled "Bartleby: Labour of Love" (May 26, 2018). The publication recognizes that "The modern economy has been immensely complex. Coordinating the production of goods and services across international supply chains represents a huge achievement. Management at all levels is probably more difficult today than ever before. So this seems an ideal moment to launch our new column."[1]

Similarly, it is worth our time to look at management in this primer as follows. First, we will define management. Second, we will examine the job of a manager. Third, we will explore what people will expect of you when you become a manager.

What Is Management?

Simply put, management is the process of coordinating resources to achieve the organization's goals. Sounds simple, right? Let's break down that definition into its component parts to see what is actually involved.

Management is a **process**, meaning there are no clear steps I can offer you as to how to manage. Each situation, each manufacturing process, each client interaction, each human resource interface, each financial instrument, each industry, each logistical component, and each problem requires a manager to deal with a unique situation. Moreover, the management process is ongoing; there is no clear beginning, middle, and end.

---

[1] The Economist. May 26, 2018. "Our New Column on Management and Work," p. 57.

Management is a process of **coordinating** all the functional areas of the firm. That's a big job. Managers are constantly juggling pieces, a skill that requires multitasking. Are you someone who can multitask? Or are you someone who likes to be given one task to accomplish at a time? Effective managers tend to be those who can juggle many pieces of the business simultaneously, using critical thinking skills to prioritize.

What are managers coordinating? **Resources**, that is, all types of resources that are required to meet the needs of a particular business at a point in time. Economists group resources into three categories to include land (i.e., physical spaces, property), labor (i.e., human resources, people), and capital (i.e., tangible, financial).

In the end, management is the process of coordinating resources in order **to achieve a specified goal.** Just because a manager is busy all day, making decisions, securing resources, mobilizing people, and coordinating activities does not mean the manager will be deemed successful. The key to success in management is achieving an agreed-upon goal. This is how you will be judged as a manager and how your year-end bonus will be determined. Before you accept a job as a manager, be sure to ask for clarity on the specific goal(s) you will be expected to achieve in the end.

Managerial Functions

The entire premise of this primer is to expose you to what businesspeople call the *functional areas of business*, the key domains that every businessperson needs to understand to be successful. Now we are going to look at what managers do all day, which in business is called "management functions." Try not to confuse these two terms—"functional areas of business" and "management functions"—as they have distinct meanings.

You get a job as a manager. Great! What are you going to be doing all day? A French mining engineer named Henri Fayol in 1888 labeled the primary functions of management as planning, organizing, commanding, coordinating, and controlling. Today, businesspeople have compressed Fayol's topology into four key management functions to suit the contemporary business environment of the 2020s: **planning, organizing, monitoring, and leading/following**, discussed in turn below.

Planning

We defined management as a process of coordinating resources to achieve a goal. The planning function suggests that we start planning based on the last part of the definition: the ultimate goal. Whatever plans we devise depend on what it means to successfully achieve the stated goal of the business.

Planning requires acute strategic formulation. A strategic business planner might ask:

- What would make our business unique?
- How could we outperform our competitors?
- What does success look like?
- What does effectiveness look like?
- How can our business play to its strengths?
- How can our business products and services be distinctive?
- What risks are worth taking and not taking?

To achieve its goals, a business must devise plans, be they strategic, tactical, or operational. *Strategic plans* are the most comprehensive type of plan and do not include details on how the business is going to achieve its goals. Rather, strategic plans present a big picture of what the business wants to look like in 5+ years.

Tactical plans present some of the nuts and bolts required to achieve the big picture as articulated in the strategic plan. Tactical plans encompass what needs to occur within a 1- to 5-year window and are presented on a smaller scale than strategic plans and thus are easier to periodically update as new information feeds into the system.

Operational plans are the most flexible because they address very specific aspects of a strategic plan that can be achieved in the short term (i.e., within 1 year) to help the business achieve its broad strategic objectives.

Organizing

Once the strategists have clarified their vision, managers charged with the organizing function go into action mode to put the plans in place. Their focus is on how to achieve the goals efficiently and effectively.

Organizational managers must think about the who, what, when, where, how, and how much.

In other words, organizational managers begin to identify and "coordinate" the pieces of the managerial process necessary to reach the firm's goals.

Monitoring

Monitoring entails overseeing the various moving parts required to put a business plan into action. Managers who assume this function are charged with assessing the degree to which the business is reaching its operational, tactical, and ultimately strategic plans. Are people doing their parts? Are there sufficient resources? Is there enough money? Do we have to make operational changes? What kinds of corrective action are advised? Are we getting closer to our goals?

In the nineteenth and twentieth centuries, managers associated the monitoring function with "controlling," which is certainly one way to manage a process. In the twenty-first century, however, managers have learned that controlling can lead to micro-management and other adverse effects that do not always bode well for the managerial process. The concept of controlling has thus been expanded to a discussion of how to monitor ongoing activities in ways that yield the best results for the business. How you monitor the business process will most likely be unique to your style, workplace, occupation, and industry.

Leading/Following

The last of the four managerial functions is leading/following, two sides of the same coin. In order to be an effective leader, one must learn how to follow. Conversely, effective followers also need to know how to lead. In business we realize there is only one chief executive officer. Most of our time will be spent learning how to be a good follower in anticipation of the day when we might be asked to lead.

Managers assuming the leadership function are charged with finding the most effective ways to motivate people to do whatever is within a staff member's means to help the business achieve its stated goals. Can you find ways as a manager to match people's skills and interests with the tasks at hand? Can you find ways to keep people satisfied and productive? Can you discover what people want to contribute to the business and then secure the necessary resources to make that happen? If so, you will contribute to the overall goals of this business.

At colleges today, there is a big push to host leadership training programs often for academic credit. It is great to be able to assume leadership with confidence and skill. However, do not be in such a hurry to leave a position in which you are very skilled to assume a supervisory position until you are ready. As the saying goes, *you may lose a good plumber and gain a lousy manager*. Think about how many times that has probably happened!

The Roles of Managers

The above managerial functions indicate what managers are doing all day: planning, organizing, monitoring, and leading/following. Now we take a look at what people will expect of you as a manager, something we call the roles of managers of which there are three: **informational, interpersonal, and decisional roles**, described in turn below.

Informational Role

Being able to put your finger on information that will help your business succeed is critical to success. Managers assuming the informational role are charged with gathering pertinent data. What do you need to know to achieve your stated goals? Where do you get good information? What is your data reconnaissance method?

Gathering information is an ongoing task for a manager. As such, it is key to read as much as you can to keep abreast of the latest in your industry, to talk to people willing to help you access relevant information, and to seek out timely information both internally in your business and in the broader business community.

Once collected, a manager then discerns what to do with the collected information. To whom should the data be disseminated? Who would benefit from having specific information? Does everyone in your business need to know everything? What is urgent? What information is not urgent?

Depending on your industry, there may be formal channels people rely upon to obtain needed information to do their jobs. Business managers may choose staff meetings or electronic messages as formal dissemination mechanisms. The choice is up to you as the manager, depending on what seems to work best with your staff.

An *informal* way to collect and disseminate information is around the water cooler (or coffee pot) where people tend to gather and chat. Informal information can be just as valuable to a business as formal information. What is your style? What kinds of information collection and dissemination have you observed on the job? What has worked? What information have you wished your manager had shared in order for you to be able to do your job better? If you are not getting adequate information, let your supervisor know. It can make a big difference in the degree to which you will be productive on the job.

Interpersonal Role

Effective management starts with you understanding yourself. Who are you? What makes you unique? What are your preferences? What do you demand of others? Self-awareness enhances our ability as managers and is learned through examination of our own values, emotional intelligence, cognition skills, adaptability, and personalities. Having a good sense of yourself is necessary to be effective with others.

A manager then branches out into the interpersonal, meaning the interaction between people in the workplace, yourself included. This is key to succeed as a manager. Being a liaison between people requires learning supportive communication techniques to understand a given situation and the people involved. Skillful communication leads to person agency (or power), the empowerment of colleagues, enhanced relationships, and an energized workplace where people can be productive.

Communication skills are twofold. First one learns to develop strong listening skills, whereby people feel truly heard by you as their manager. This entails focusing the mind on what the person in front of you is trying to communicate without distraction. Effecting listening requires being quiet and not talking. This is not easy or automatic but can be developed with practice and in time. Second, effective communication requires one to learn supportive speaking techniques that empower you and your colleagues.

When employed effectively, supportive communication results in people being able to express their ideas with confidence to engender openness and trust in the workplace. Supportive communication also can be used to correct behaviors, deliver negative feedback, or point out someone's shortcoming. The overall goal is to enhance the interpersonal relationships within the workplace—through supportive listening and speaking—while tackling whatever difficult issue needs to be discussed.

Managers may be asked to play an interpersonal role outside their business, say in the community. This entails participating in community events as a figurehead for your business. Think of ribbon-cutting ceremonies, heralding a new building or a new community center where the chief executive of a business has a pair of scissors in hand to cut the ribbon for the camera. External interpersonal managerial skills are just as important as internal interpersonal skills.

Decisional Role

The last role managers may be asked to play is the decisional role. This is when a person has been granted authority to make decisions for the business that will impact how successfully a business achieves its goals.

A fancy title, however, does not always come with decision-making authority. Often in my work in the Arab world, I have seen highly educated women with important-looking titles who actually had little to no power. They were never given any authority to make decisions. Thus, it might be valuable to look below the surface of your culture to see who gets to make decisions. Whether you are being asked to be a manager or are joining a new business, find out who the decision makers are, who will be able to help you succeed.

The three managerial roles—informational, interpersonal and decisional—are interconnected if we consider what managers have in common. A manager vested with authority over an organizational unit is granted status that leads to the kinds of interpersonal relations that lead to access to information that enables the manager to make strategic decisions. Thus, while you may be asked to wear one of the managerial hats, over time you may see yourself wearing all three.

Wrap Up

Management—the process of coordinating resources to achieve a goal—is a challenging but potentially rewarding job. The challenge goes beyond knowing how to establish plans, secure financial resources, design a production process, as well as working endless hours every day. Management requires adroit skills in communicating with people, be they members of the board of directors, suppliers, financiers, subcontractors, employees, customers, or the general public. And perhaps the skills learned to be an effective manager may spill over into your personal life and serve you in additional ways.

Hence, my recommendation is to take courses in human development, psychology, and management in college before you start a career in business. If you are smart, hardworking, and inquisitive, you will probably be tapped to become a manager or supervisor someday, at which time these managerial skills and knowledge will serve you well.

References

BDP International. 2019. "Global Locations." https://www.bdpinternational.com/locations.

Bernays, E. 1923. *Crystallizing Public Opinion*. New York, NY: Boni and Leveright.

Bhattarai, A. May 25, 2018. "Does Walmart Take the Shine Off Its High-End Acquisitions?" *Seattle Times*, https://snewsi.com/id/18273629197.

Blum, A. 2012. *Tubes: A Journey to the Center of the Internet*. New York, NY: HarperCollins Publishers.

CNBC. August 1, 2017. "Snap Is Falling again as Wall Street Worries about the Company's Corporate Structure." https://www.cnbc.com/2017/08/01/snapchat-excluded-from-sp-500-what-does-it-mean.html.

Cruikshank, J.L., and A.W. Schultz. 2010. *The Man Who Sold America: The Amazing (But True!) Story of Albert D. Lasker and the Creation of the Advertising Century*. Boston, MA: Harvard Business Review.

Einstein, M. 2016. *Black Ops Advertising: Native Ads, Content Marketing, and the Covert World of the Digital Sell*. New York, NY: OR Books.

Equilar. August 25, 2017. "Highest-Paid CFOs Exceed $20 Million in Total Compensation." https://www.equilar.com/blogs/299-highest-paid-cfos-2016.html.

Ewen, S. 1996. *PR! A Social History of Spin*. New York, NY: Basic.

Fitzgerald, D., and B. Kendall. April 16, 2019. "T-Mobile-Sprint Dean Runs into Resistance from DOJ Anti-trust Staff," *The Wall Street Journal*. https://www.wsj.com/articles/t-mobile-sprint-deal-runs-into-resistance-from-doj-antitrust-staff-11555446461?mod=e2tw.

Flynn, P. 2017. "Autonomous Humanoid Robots as a Pedagogical Platform in the Business Classroom." *Journal of Social Science Studies* 4, no. 1, pp. 178–188.

Ford, H. 1926. *Today and Tomorrow*. New York, NY: Productivity Press.

Franchise Direct. February 19, 2019. "Top 100 Global Franchises 2019." https://www.franchisedirect.com/top100globalfranchises/rankings.

Gartner. 2018. "Gartner's 2018 Annual Report on Cloud Computing." https://www.gartner.com/en/products/special-reports.

Hoffman, B. 2012. *American Icon: Alan Mulally and the Fight to Save Ford Motor Company*. New York, NY: Crown Business.

Investment News. August 1, 2017. "Assets at RIAs Growing at 5.8%," p. 3.

Kotler, P., and G. Zaltman. July, 1971. "Social Marketing: An Approach to Planned Social Change." *Journal of Marketing* 35, pp. 3–12.

Hodgson, C. May 8, 2018. "HSBC Rolls Out Facial Recognition for Mobile." *The Financial Times*, https://www.ft.com/content/acc823c0-52a6-11e8-b3ee-41e0209208ec.

Hodgson, C., and P. Waldmeir. May 9, 2018. "Airlines Seek to Lift Profit Margins with Big Data." *The Financial Times*, p. 27.

Mims, C. April, 2017. "Three Difficult Lessons for Traditional Retailers." *The Wall Street Journal*, p. B1-B2.

McCarthy, E.J. 1960. *Basic Marketing: A Managerial Approach*. Homewood, IL: R.D. Irwin.

Milne, R. October 12, 2016. "Norway's Oil Fund Warns over Lack of IPOs." *The Financial Times*, p. 14.

Murray, A. November, 2017. "China's Singles Day Is a Shopping Extravaganza Heard around the World." *Time Inc*. https://www.scribd.com/article/364746736/China-S-Singles-Day-Is-A-Shopping-Extravaganza-Heard-Around-The-World.

Oxfam America. April 14, 2016. *Broken at the Top: How America's Dysfunctional Tax System Costs Billions in Corporate Tax Dodging*.

Oxfam America. April 12, 2017. *Rigged Reform: US Companies Are Dodging Billions in Taxes but Proposed Reforms will Make Things Worse*.

Pallotta, D. June 15, 2011. "A Logo Is Not a Brand." Boston, MA: Harvard Business Review. https://hbr.org/2011/06/a-logo-is-not-a-brand.

Parrish, J.R. December 12, 2017. "Real-Estate Firms Look to Technology to Figure out Shoppers." http://jrparrish.com/real-estate-firms-look-to-technology-to-figure-out-shoppers.

Piore, A. January/February, 2018. "The Surgeon Who Wants to Connect You to the Internet with a Brain Implant." *MIT Technology Review* 121, no. 1, pp. 45–59.

Roberts, D. May 7, 2018. "Wells Fargo Knows Customers Are Still Frustrated. Here's What They're Doing about It." *The Charlotte Observer*, p. C1.

Shenkar, O. 2010. *Copycats: How Smart Companies Use Imitation to Gain a Strategic Edge*. Boston, MA: Harvard Business Press.

Small Business Administration (SBA). 2019. *Learning Center for Online and Face-to-Face Courses*. https://www.sba.gov/tools/sba-learning-center/search/training.

The Economist. September 14, 2019. "Chips with Everything," p.13.

The Economist. January 20, 2018. "Business," p. 9.

The Economist. January 6, 2018. "Ant Financial and MoneyGram Blocked Transfer," p. 46.

The Economist. January 6, 2018. "The Year of the Incumbent," p. 49.

The Economist. May 26, 2018. "Our New Column on Management and Work," p. 57.

The Economist. June 15, 2017. "German Deep Discounters Go Big in America," p. 122.

The Economist. September 9, 2017. "Visual Computing: The Facial-Industrial Complex," p. 83.

The Economist. October 28, 2017. "Apple Capital LLC," p. 65.

The Economist. October 28, 2017. "E-Commerce: There Be Giants," p. 31.

The Economist. November 11, 2017. "The Internet of Things: Bish Bash Bosch," p. 59.

The Economist. May 28, 2016. "Online Platforms: Nostrums for Rostrums," p. 111.

The Economist. September 24, 2016. "Tata Group: Mistry's Elephant," p. 23.

The Economist. January 7, 2012. "The Drug Industry: Battling Borderless Bugs," p. 55.

The Economist. June 23, 2012. "African Entrepreneurs: Parallel Players," p. 69.

The Economist. March 5, 2011. "The Tata Group: Out of India," pp. 75–77.

The Financial Times. September 2-3, 2017. "Sensors and Sensibility: How Citi Tracks Desk Use," p. 27.

The Times of India. May 22, 2010. "Abbott Buys Piramal's Pharma Arm for $3.7bn," https://timesofindia.indiatimes.com/business/india-business/Abbott-buys-Piramals-pharma-arm-for-3-7bn/articleshow/5960176.cms.

The Wall Street Journal. October 17, 2016. "Investors Unfazed by Borrowing Increase," p. B3.

The Wall Street Journal. February 16, 2018. "Rise of Private Assets Is Built on Mountain of Debt," p. B1.

The Wall Street Journal. February 16, 2018. "Regulator Targets Firms with Dual-Class Shares," p. B1.

The World Bank. January, 2019. Doing Business 2019. Washington, DC: International Bank for Reconstruction and Development.

Tufekci, Z. 2017. Twitter and Tear Gas: The Power and Fragility of Networked Protest. New Haven, CT: Yale University Press.

Turow, J. 2017. The Aisles Have Eyes. New Haven, CT: Yale University Press.

U.S. Department of Labor. Bureau of Labor Statistics. 2019. North American Industry Classification System (NAICS). https://www.census.gov/eos/www/naics/.

U.S. Internal Revenue Services (IRS). 2019. Statistics of Income Bulletins. www.IRS.gov/taxstats.

United Nations Conference on Trade and Development. 2019. World Investment Report. New York, NY: United Nations.

Vaidhyanathan, S. 2018. Anti-Social Media: How Facebook Disconnects Us and Undermines Democracy. Oxford, England: Oxford University Press.

Wu, T. February 16, 2018. "The Tyranny of Convenience." The New York Times, https://www.nytimes.com/2018/02/16/opinion/sunday/tyranny-convenience.html.

Zuboff, S. 2019. Age of Surveillance Capitalism: The Fight for a Human Future at the New Frontier of Power. New York, NY: PublicAffairs.

About the Author

Patrice Flynn is a Fulbright scholar, University of Chicago-trained professor of business and economics, and the Morrison professor of international studies at Mount St. Mary's University (est. 1808). Her research across five continents examines global capitalism, labor markets, civil society, and autonomous humanoid robots. She is the editor of the _Working Papers Series in International Studies_ and coeditor of _Calvert-Henderson Quality of Life Indicators_ and _Measuring the Impact of the Nonprofit Sector_. Previous positions include vice president for research at Independent Sector, senior vice president for administration and finance at Effat University, and CEO/president of Flynn Research in Washington, DC, during which time she was selected as one of Lifetime Television's Women of the Year.

Index

FORTHCOMING TITLE IN BUSINESS CAREER DEVELOPMENT COLLECTION

Vilma Barr, *Editor*

- *Be Different!: The Key to Business and Career Success* by Stanley W. Silverman

Announcing the Business Expert Press Digital Library

Concise e-books business students need for classroom and research

This book can also be purchased in an e-book collection by your library as

- a one-time purchase,
- that is owned forever,
- allows for simultaneous readers,
- has no restrictions on printing, and
- can be downloaded as PDFs from within the library community.

Our digital library collections are a great solution to beat the rising cost of textbooks. E-books can be loaded into their course management systems or onto students' e-book readers.

The **Business Expert Press** digital libraries are very affordable, with no obligation to buy in future years. For more information, please visit **www.businessexpertpress.com/librarians**. To set up a trial in the United States, please email **sales@businessexpertpress.com**.

CPSIA information can be obtained
at www.ICGtesting.com
Printed in the USA
FSHW020328120120
65835FS